Praise

"Tennis Beyond Big Shots is one of the most unique books I've read. Greg not only gives players sound instruction and strategy for becoming better players on the court, but he also combines that with meaningful, welcome advice on how to be a better person off it. A must for every player's library."
CHRIS EVERT, 18-time Grand Slam Singles Champion

"Whether your aspirations are to be the next club champion or world #1, tennis is more a game of the mind than the muscles. In fact, Greg's book could be a blueprint for how I've approached the game from my junior days in Sweden through my career on the professional and senior tours. Tennis Beyond Big Shots offers instruction that will truly, and permanently improve your game."
MATS WILANDER, Former No.1 Player in the World

"You can win more matches simply by making small changes, Greg shows you how."
CLIFF DRYSDALE, Former World Top Ten Player and ESPN TV Tennis Analyst

"Want to win more and have a great time doing it? This is the book for you. Greg's book is educational, entertaining and guaranteed to make you a better player the next time you take the court."
STANLEY MATTHEWS JR., Davis Cup Star

"I wish I had written this myself! A real winner for players of all levels."
TOM GULLIKSON, Former U.S. Davis Cup Captain and coach of Pete Sampras

"This book nails it! If our world is dominated by the clock, then set yours earlier each day until you have completed Greg's book. Every player, parent and coach will benefit from having done so. Tennis is an enjoyable lifetime experience with Greg's approach. Read this book!"
GEOFF NORTON, Director of Development, Professional Tennis Registry

"Greg's made me a champion. Having not played tennis in high school and college, I was an athlete (soccer and lacrosse) not a tennis player. Working with Greg improved my technique and knowledge, but much more important, my love of the game. His coaching has made me club champion for three consecutive years."
 BOB MITCHELL, Co-President of Mitchells, Richards, Marshs

"Ball-striking has now overcome movement in the game of tennis, and most of the artistic and strategic elements of the game have been removed. Greg Moran's book gives many of the answers and solutions needed for players of all levels to see tennis at a much deeper level."
CHUCK KREISE, Men's Head Coach, Clemson University

"This book is for tennis players at every level as well as coaches, parents, and even those looking to become players. Each chapter is loaded with great anecdotes and memorable quotes. Greg has written a great and meaningful book."
BILL MOUNFORD, Director of Tennis, USTA National Tennis Center

"While reading Greg Moran's new book, I found myself smiling and nodding in agreement the whole time. It's

well written, positive, simple, and powerful . . . wonderful insights."
WAYNE BRYAN, Tennis coach and father of World No.1 Doubles team Bob & Mike Bryan

"Tennis Beyond Big Shots is a must read! I've had the pleasure of knowing Greg Moran for over twenty years and he is positive, passionate, and has helped me, and thousands like me, to not only play better tennis but to make the game one of the best parts of our lives."
JACK MITCHELL, Author of Hug Your Customers

"Tennis Beyond Big Shots offers an approach to tennis that players can absorb and apply immediately. Greg makes the game fun and since he began working with members of my team, we've moved from the bottom of our division to the top."
FRAN LENICH, USTA Team Captain

An Important Message to Our Readers

Tennis
BEYOND
Big Shots

Greg Moran

Mansion Grove House

Tennis Beyond Big Shots
Copyright © 2006 Greg Moran
Published by Mansion Grove House

ISBN 1932421041

Mansion Grove House. Box 201734, Austin, TX 78720 USA.
Website: mansiongrovehouse.com
For information on bulk purchases, custom editions and serial rights:
E-mail sales@mansiongrovehouse.com or write us, Attention: Special Sales
For permission license including reprints, excerpts and quotes: E-mail
permissions@mansiongrovehouse.com or write us, Attention: Permissions

Printed in the United States of America
Library of Congress Cataloging-in-Publication Data
Moran, Greg,
  Tennis beyond big shots / Greg Moran.
    p. cm.
  Includes bibliographical references and index.
  ISBN 1-932421-04-1 (pbk. : alk. paper)
  1. Tennis. I. Title.
  GV995.M544 2006
  796.342--dc22
                              2006008882

Tennis Beyond Big Shots Team!
Copy Editor: **Pamela Garrett**
Cover Designer: **Bill Carson**
Cover Model: **Greg Moran**
Cover Photo Shoot: **Scott Hazelwood**
Illustrator: **Richard Catron**
Permissions, Reviews & Design: **Maureen Malliaras**
Project Coordinator: **Uday Kumar**
Research & Collateral Development: **Laura Duncan**

Credits: See Appendix "Credits"

Contents

About Greg

Greg Moran brings to this book a wealth of experience spanning decades as a competitive player and much-sought-after tennis teaching professional. Award-winning Pro and Director of Tennis at The Four Seasons Racquet Club in Wilton, CT, Greg enthusiastically teaches top-ranked players, weekend warriors and eager beginners. A prolific contributing writer for leading tennis magazines, he also shares his winning strategies on television. Greg is a member of the Wilson Advisory Staff and a National Speaker for the Cardio Tennis program launched by the US Tennis Association and the Tennis Industry Association.

To

Kelley, Mike & Katie
Who mean more to me than anything...even tennis

Common Acronyms

ACC: Atlantic Coast Conference
ITF: International Tennis Federation
NASA: National Aeronautics and Space Administration
PTR: Professional Tennis Registry
USPTA: United States Professional Tennis Association
USTA: United States Tennis Association
YMCA: Young Men's Christian Association

Introduction

The New Power Game

We live in a world that glorifies power. Be it on the battlefield, in the boardroom or classroom and, yes, on the tennis court, power equals winning. Power turns us on, and nowhere is this more apparent than in the way we live our lives.

The bedside alarm jolts us awake and the race begins! We jump out of bed, take a "power" shower, skip breakfast, and then sprint for the next 15 hours. Work, school, errands, lunch on the run. And God forbid we get stuck behind a truck and are late for our next very important "power" meeting.

Dominated by the clock, our minds are constantly racing while our bodies struggle to keep up. We take great pride in telling each other how hectic our schedules are and how little sleep we get, though we do try to squeeze in a "power" nap. At the end of the day, physically and emotionally spent, we collapse into bed only to do it all again tomorrow.

Not surprisingly, we bring this same frenzied, hard-hitting approach to our tennis lives. In today's game, Power Tennis means big shots: 100-mph serves and rocket-propelled forehands. Crunch those service returns and you'll feel just like Agassi. One big winner and victory is within your reach...game, set, and match? Well, not so fast!

Thirty-five years as a player, teaching professional and writer have shown me that the big shot approach to tennis seldom wins matches. In fact, it usually produces frustration, injury and can even drive players away from the game forever.

Welcome to the New Power Tennis! Tennis Beyond Big Shots contains simple, smart, bold lessons and strategies guaranteed to make you a better tennis player the next time you step onto the court. You'll come to realize that power that doesn't focus on big shots can be more devastating to your opponents than a 130-mph serve.

I've taught the working warriors, as well as those whose sole goal is to rise to the top of their 3.0 leagues. I've worked with the highly ranked players, the junior who's dying to make his high school team, and I've seen the light in the eyes of the 7-year-old deaf girl with Down Syndrome as she watches her first forehand fly over the net. Whatever your tennis goals, I will help you achieve them, and more.

Tennis Beyond Big Shots is not an A to Z book on tennis, but rather a treasure chest of proven plans to help you win more matches and make tennis one of the most enjoyable parts of your life.

In Part 1, I offer you four easy-to-follow strategies that will improve your game right away. Part 2 will get a bit more specific and touch on strokes, but I promise, no major grip or swing changes. You don't need them. You'll see how you can become a better player with the strokes you now have.

Part 3 is a progressive approach to strategy that will guide you through your matches and beyond. Whether you're working with a teaching professional or are self-taught, the information in Parts 1-3 will build on where you are now and take your game to the next level, fast

A long life of enjoyable tennis is everyone's goal. However, when you participate in the world of social tennis, there are usually a few bad bounces along the way. In Part 4 we'll take a look at the 10 commandments of social tennis, guaranteed to make you one of the most sought after players at your club.

Each chapter has its own message, so whether you have several hours on an airplane or a few minutes between sets, you'll find the book reader friendly. I've also sprinkled in some quotes I've found to be particularly enlightening. I hope that after reading this book, you'll keep it close by to use as a consistent reference throughout the rest of your tennis life.

Since being given the gift of tennis as a child, the game has been a major part of my life. I was a ranked junior, a high school "star," played on a pretty good college team and even met my wife on the tennis court. Along the way, I've learned that tennis is a sport for life that can be enjoyed on many levels and for many reasons: competition, exercise, camaraderie or just for the pure joy of hitting the ball. Ultimately, tennis is a treasure that can be passed on to the next generation.

Whether you dream of winning Wimbledon, rising to the top of your club ladder or just want to hit the ball and have a great time, Tennis Beyond Big Shots will make you feel like a champion, on and off the court.

Greg Moran
Greg_Moran@TennisBeyondBigShots.com

Part 1

Small Changes
To Win Big

Over the past few years, tennis instruction has become so complicated and power oriented that you need to be a physicist to understand it and a contortionist to apply it. We're led to believe that new age technique and big shots are needed so that we can compete in what is now mysteriously called the "modern game."

A student of mine, Frank (not his real name), is a classic victim of this. Frank is forever trying the latest grip, stroke or big shot strategy in an attempt to move his game to the next level. He takes to the court each week and proceeds to fire away. As ball after ball hits the side of his racket, burns a hole in the net or flies over the baseline, he squeezes his grip a little bit tighter and keeps swinging away.

When he begins to feel that slight twinge of pain in his elbow, he simply pops a few pills and continues swinging as hard as he can...just in case one happens to go in.

Oh, Frank does manage to hit the occasional "world class" shot and, when he does, he's on top of the world. He wins the point, everyone around bows to his "greatness" and, for that brief moment, Frank's wife loves him just a little bit more.

This ever so occasional brush with the stars is just enough to keep him flailing away. Oblivious to the 20-30 errors that sandwich his "great" shots, Frank also fails to see that his approach to the game might have something to do with his five consecutive first- round losses in his club championship.

The fact is, in most cases, new age technique and big shots are not necessary to win more tennis matches. With a few minor adjustments, a little discipline and a good plan, the skills you now have will be more than enough to take you to the next level and beyond.

Chapter 1

Big Shots
Are For Wimps

Power is the ultimate aphrodisiac," said former Secretary of State Henry Kissinger. In tennis, this is more apparent than ever. Put the word "power" in front of anything, and we'll rush to buy it. Power rackets, power strings, power shoes, power warm-ups, you name it. If it's got the word "power" on it, we want it.

To the recreational athlete, power is the mark of a good tennis player, and it's easy to understand why. We see Andy Roddick fire in a 150-mph serve or watch Maria Sharapova hit a forehand that would penetrate concrete, and we walk away thinking that winning tennis is all about big shots and quick points.

Power looks good and it feels great. Few things on a tennis court get the juices flowing like ripping a winner past your lunging opponent. The problem comes when the search for those "magic moments" dominates our style of play.

"Hit it harder!" "Blast 'em off the court!" "Go for broke!"

These are the phrases that come to mind when I think of today's recreational players. Encouraged by television and technology, Average Joe tennis player walks onto the court armed with a super-charged racket and a hit-big-to-win-big attitude. As ball after ball hits the net, fence, or players on the next court, Joe's frustration level rises and his blood begins to boil. For Joe, "hit big to win big" usually meant "hit big to lose quickly."

Sound familiar? Sure it does. There are millions of players just like Joe who approach tennis with a power-is-king attitude. While there is a place for power in your tennis game, it is not your biggest weapon—not even close.

The foundation of a winning tennis player is not power and aggression but consistency and control. From here on out, I want you to forget about the "hit-'em-as-hard-as-you-can" mentality. It's a waste of time and a recipe for disaster.

I'm going to help you develop a style of shotmaking and strategy that will allow you to win points with what's between your ears, rather than what you're holding in your hand. Before we get into specifics, here's an overview of the way your game is going to evolve:

It all begins with consistency

Several times a week, a player comes to me upset about their latest loss to someone they feel they "should have beaten easily." The conversation usually goes something like this:

Greg: *"How did your game go?"*

Anne: *"Terrible. I lost, and the girl I played*
                stunk. All she did was get the ball
                back."

Greg: *"All she did was get the ball*
(to myself)   *back? Hello? Isn't that the*
                idea?"

In today's big shot world, the ability to "just" get the ball back has somehow become something to be looked down upon. Those who "just get the ball back" have been

Hit it as hard as you can... in case it goes in.

thrown in with the other black sheep of the tennis world, the "lobbers," "pushers" and "dinkers." Macho tennis players call these people "tennis wimps." You know what I call them? Winners!

To develop into a winning tennis player, you must first and foremost become consistent with all of your shots. This means being able to keep the ball down the center of the court with as much ease as you unzip your racket bag.

> *Consistency is a mental weapon.*
>
> Nick Bollettieri
> World Class coach

Consistency is the foundation on which the rest of your game will be built, and if you can learn to keep the ball in play you'll always be a tough opponent.

Power thrills but placement kills

These words, spoken by Chuck Kriese, the winningest tennis coach in Atlantic Coast Conference history, say it all. The winner of a tennis match is seldom the player who can hit the ball the hardest, but rather the one who can place the ball where they want on a consistent basis.

Once you've developed the ability to keep the ball in the court, your next goal is to work on your placement. You need to be able to hit the ball to each side of the court, down the middle, deep in the court and, on occasion, short in the court.

Tennis legend Andre Agassi has become a master at this. Known for his penetrating groundstrokes, Agassi's opponents frequently find themselves scrambling well behind the baseline as they struggle to handle his deep shots to both corners. When Andre tosses in a soft drop shot, all they can do is watch helplessly as the ball gently floats over the net, out of their reach.

I personally, and somewhat painfully, learned the importance of consistency and placement when I had the special opportunity to practice with Wojtek Fibak. Fibak, the great Polish professional, was once ranked as high as No. 13 in the world and won 48 titles on the pro tour during a solid 13-year career. He was the real deal.

As we played points, I noticed that Fibak didn't hit the ball particularly hard, but he rarely missed a shot and his control was tremendous: Deep, short, you name it. He could place the ball on a dime. The majority of his shots landed 1-2 feet inside my baseline. Deep, to say the least. If I couldn't keep my shots at that same depth, the point was over. Not right away, though.

Fibak never went for spectacular winners, but if I gave him even one ball that he could step into, he took immediate control of the point and began moving me all over the court. He gradually took me apart, and it was just a matter of time before I collapsed, from either exhaustion or impatience, and missed or gave him something he could easily put away.

Use Spin to Win

Once you've developed consistency and control, your next task is to learn to put various types of spin on the ball. By learning to hit slice using a high-to-low racket path and low- to-high topspin, you'll enhance both your consistency and control and, at the same time, make it more difficult for your opponents to control their shots.

Consistency, placement and spin - with these weapons at your disposal, you'll be able to keep the ball in play and move your opponents around the court. After a few shots, you'll often frustrate them to the point where they'll simply lose their patience and try to end the point quickly with a big shot. You can then smile to yourself as that big shot sails over the baseline or into the net, handing you another point.

But when do I get to rip it?

I know, I know. You're dying to hit the ball hard, but I purposely left power out of my progression of skills because, at this point in the book, I want you to focus on these other, much more crucial areas of your game. I want you to first learn to play what famed tennis journalist Bud Collins calls "athletic chess."

For many players, the big-shot, quick-kill approach is the "wimpy" way out. It's much easier to take a big swing at the ball, hoping to hit an outright winner, than it is to develop the skill and determination to hang in there and construct a point.

We'll get into power later, but for now work on becoming a consistent player who can place shots to all areas of the court. I think you'll find that these weapons will prove much more "powerful" than the occasional "big shot."

Here are three drills, ones I've done for thirty years, that will help you improve both your consistency and control. All you need is a practice partner and two tennis ball cans.

1. Place one can in the center of the court, three feet inside the baseline. Have your practice partner do the same. Rally back and forth, each of you trying to hit the other's can.
2. Move the cans into the forehand court, three feet inside the baseline and three feet inside the singles sideline. Again, try to hit each other's can.
3. Move the cans to the same spot on the backhand side of the court and try to knock the cans over.

Yes, at the professional level the game is extremely fast and power is an important element, but until Venus or Andre calls you for a match, build your game around consistency and control and you'll see an immediate improvement in your results.

BOBBY RIGG'S AIRTIGHT TENNIS

Though best remembered for his loss to Billie Jean King in the 1973 "Battle of the Sexes"—the most-watched match in tennis history—Bobby Riggs was much more than the chauvinistic hustler he portrayed in that drama. He was, in reality, one heck of a tennis player!

Riggs dominated the amateur, professional and senior games. He liked to say that from the age of 13 to age 76, he was the best tennis player in the world for his age. Along the way he played against and defeated legends like Bill Tilden and Don Budge. He was ranked No. 1 in the world in 1939. He won Wimbledon once and Forest Hills (now the U.S. Open) twice and was three times U.S. Professional Champion.

Riggs was a player known for his exquisite touch and movement, a player who was a tenacious competitor and a terrific strategist. He made a career out of outsmarting bigger, stronger opponents. His coach, Esther Bartosh, taught him very early on that "tennis matches are won on mistakes." The important thing for Riggs was to not miss the ball. Let the other fellow hit the ball too hard. Let the other fellow hit the ball into the net. Let the other fellow make the mistakes. The most important lesson was that it's not how hard you hit the ball, but where you hit it.

Riggs took his coach's words to heart. He called this style of play "airtight tennis," and for more than 60 years frustrated opponents with his consistency, change of pace, spin and, above all, mental toughness. You can, too.

Chapter 2

Keep It Simple And Win

The advice is endless: bring your racket back this way, follow through that way, use a big loop, a semi-loop, roll your wrist, lock your wrist, open stance, closed stance, blah, blah, blah. There are more theories about hitting a tennis ball than there are flavors at Baskin-Robbins.

Hitting a tennis ball is just not that complicated. In fact, I can sum it up for you with what I like to call the four Rs:

1. Read the ball
2. Ready your racket
3. Run to the ball
4. Rotate your body

Now wait! Stop rolling your eyes and hear me out.

You're undoubtedly thinking, "It can't be that simple. Where's the high-tech?" Well, it is that simple, and tennis is not a high-tech game. It's a game of basics, and by focusing on these basics you'll jump to the next level faster than you can say Martina Navratilova.

Read the ball

It's tough to hit a moving object, so your first task is to figure out where the ball is going once it leaves your opponent's strings. You do this by both watching and listening as the ball is struck

Cut out the fancy thinking and just concentrate on mastering the fundamentals and you'll beat most of the players who beat you now.

Vic Braden
World-renowned tennis teacher

Watch it

Though "watch the ball" is the first tip most of us ever received, it will always be the game's most important piece of advice. It's also the most difficult to follow on a consistent basis because there's a lot going on around us. The wind and sun, not to mention the pretty girl or guy on the next court, can all be distracting.

I want you to develop "ball vision," which means that once the point begins, you look at nothing but the ball. Don't worry about watching your opponent or their racket. If you're focusing on the ball, both will eventually come into the picture.

Watch it from the moment the server holds it in his hand. As he tosses the ball, keep your head still and follow it with your eyes. As he makes contact, see which direction the ball travels when it leaves his strings and immediately say to yourself "forehand," or "backhand."

> *Watch the ball as though it may disappear at any moment.*
>
> Pancho Gonzalez
> Two-time U.S. National champion

Notice the height of the ball as it crosses the net. Watch the seams of the ball as it bounces and travels that last two to three feet into your strings. Follow it as it flies back over to your opponent's side of the court.

Bill Mountford, the Director of Tennis at the National Tennis Center in Flushing, New York, suggests the following exercise to help improve your ball watching technique. "Find a target that is close to you and then one off in the distance," says Bill. "Stare at the near target, and then switch your gaze to the target further away. It will take a moment to readjust your vision. The more that you practice this, the less time it takes to readjust."

Teaching Professional Scott Ford has a great DVD on the market called Welcome to the Zone (More info:

arete-sports.com) to help our visual and, in turn, our mental focus on the court.

Here are three of my favorite ball-watching exercises:

1.   Stand at the baseline and have a friend or ball machine randomly feed you balls from the baseline on the opposite side of the court. As soon as you can, yell out "forehand" or "backhand." Try to identify the shot before the ball crosses the net. After 40-50 balls, switch sides and become the feeder as your partner tries to pick up your shots.

2.   Take some old tennis balls and a red magic marker. Write numbers on each ball and have a friend feed the balls to you. As the ball approaches, don't try to hit it but rather call out the number on the ball as soon as you can.

3.   You and a partner start off on the service lines and begin softly rallying back and forth within the service lines. After a few shots, put a second ball in play and try to keep both going. This will force your eyes to be alert and constantly adjust. After a while, move back to the baseline and continue the drill.

Don't forget to listen to the ball

The importance of listening to the ball is seldom discussed but is a vital part of reading your opponent's shot. By paying attention to the sound as the ball strikes your opponent's racket, you can pick up how hard or soft it's been hit, if it's been hit with excessive spin or if it's been mis-hit. Each has its own distinctive sound.

A hard hit ball sounds like a big "boom" while a ball hit softly sounds more like a "tap." A ball that's been hit with excessive spin makes a "hissing" sound" and a mis-hit shot bears that unmistakable, irritating noise that I often compare to fingernails running down a blackboard.

By watching and listening to the ball you'll pick up cues as to where your opponent's shot is going to bounce and what it's going to do after it lands. You can then respond accordingly. For example, if you see that the ball is three feet or higher above the net and booms as if it's been hit hard, you need to immediately begin backing up. Conversely, if the ball comes off your opponent's racket less than three feet over the net and the sound is softer, like a gentle tap, you need to quickly start moving forward.

If you hear the sound of spin—hiss—and see that your opponent has swung with a low to high motion, they've hit with topspin, which means that when the ball bounces it will quickly jump towards you. If you hear the hiss and the swing was a high to low motion that means slice, which will cause the ball to stay low or even die as it hits the court.

If you're opponent has mis-hit their shot—ugh... fingernails on the blackboard—it's very difficult to determine which way the ball will dance after it bounces. If at all possible, try to move forward and take it in the air so you won't have to deal with the unpredictable spin that the mis-hit puts on the ball.

If you can't reach the ball in time and must let it bounce, get to the spot where you anticipate it will land as quickly as possible and be prepared for it to jump one way or the other. Most of the time, you'll be able to react quickly enough to get the ball back in play.

The importance of hearing the ball as it's struck has recently been in the headlines as Serena Williams and Maria Sharapova, two players who grunt loudly as they hit their shots, have drawn complaints from their opponents. Beyond disrupting their concentration, their opponents claim the grunting also hinders their ability to hear the ball being hit.

Sharapova, nicknamed the "Queen of Screams," grunts so loudly that her on-court noises were once measured by an English tabloid at 101 decibels. That's roughly the same level of sound you'd hear if you were standing next to a revved up motorcycle.

The next time you play, put on a pair of earmuffs or stuff some cotton in your ears. You'll be amazed at how important hearing the ball is for your preparation.

Ready Your Racket

Once you've determined which shot you'll need to play, ready your racket with a lightning-fast shoulder turn.

A major mistake among many recreational players is late racket preparation. To avoid this, I tell my students to get their racket positioned as quickly as they possibly can. As a goal, try to have your racket in position before your opponent's shot crosses the net.

Initially, it may feel a bit awkward to get your racket moving this quickly. Players will sometimes complain, "It messes up my timing." It does not "mess up" your timing, it changes it. Believe me, you'll be able to adjust your timing, and when you do, you'll find that you're going to have far more time to execute your shot. There is no such thing as "too soon" in racket preparation and if your racket is prepared, you'll always be able to take a good swing at the ball.

The next time you get a chance to watch Venus or Serena Williams play, pay special attention to how fast they prepare their rackets. The moment their opponent strikes the ball, it looks as if their rackets have been shot out of a cannon.

How you bring your racket back is up to you. Most of today's stars use some type of a circular or "loop" backswing, feeling that it's more rhythmic and conducive to topspin and power. Legends like Jimmy Connors and Chris Evert preferred more of a straight back motion. I suggest you use both, depending upon how much time you have to prepare.

Far more important than the style of your backswing is the size of your backswing. How high and far you take your racket back is determined by two factors: where you are in the court and how fast the ball is coming towards you. When you're not rushed, follow these three general rules:

- Take a full backswing at the baseline.
- Take a half backswing at the service line.
- Use no backswing at the net.

Be sure to also factor in the speed of your opponent's shot. If you're at the baseline and your opponent has hit a hard shot toward you, you may not have time for a full backswing. Just get the racket out in front of your body as quickly as possible. Point your strings toward your target and squeeze your grip tight so that the pace of the oncoming ball won't cause it to shift in your hands.

If you're faced with a slow-moving ball at the service line, you can use a larger backswing in preparation for a bigger swing. At the net, don't use any backswing. Simply move forward and push your racket toward the ball.

Run to the ball

As you prepare your racket, you should simultaneously get your feet moving for the obvious reason that if you don't get to the ball you won't be able to hit it. We've all heard the term "happy feet" to describe footwork. "Happy" to me means relaxed and mellow. I want my students to have "angry" feet because anger conveys intensity and that's what you need to have good footwork.

Jimmy Connors, who holds the record for the most singles titles (109) in men's tennis history, had "angry" feet. I'll never forget the first time I heard Jimmy practice. That's right, I said "heard." I was approaching the court where Connors was working out and heard a noise that can only be described as the sound one hears just before a major car accident—rubber on pavement, stopping short, over and over again.

Connors' feet were working so hard—stopping, pushing off, moving to the ball, pivoting—that his sneakers were squeaking on the court like a drag racer's tires! It looked as if Jimmy was trying to stomp the paint right off the tennis court. The rumor back then was that Connors went through over 300 pairs of shoes each year. Now that's what you call burning rubber!

Many stroking errors are a result of poor footwork. With that in mind, we'll look at footwork in depth in the next chapter, but for now remember that your ultimate goal is to be in position, with your racket ready, before the ball arrives.

Find your strike zone

The most important element of hitting a tennis ball is preparation, with the goal being to hit the ball in your "strike zone." For most players hitting groundstrokes, this means in front of your body and between your waist and knees. When hitting volleys, the strike zone is around shoulder height for most players.

This is considered your strike zone because in this area your shoulders, hips, trunk and legs can move your racket and provide power while your arm and wrist control your racket face and, therefore, your shot.

When you're able to hit the ball inside your strike zone, it's much easier to execute a controlled stroke. If you get caught having to hit outside of this area, either due to a strong shot by your opponent or poor preparation, your arm then has to work harder to move the racket and generate power. This makes it far more difficult to control your racket head and also puts additional stress on your arm.

Footwork is vital to hitting the ball in your strike zone because, unfortunately, our opponents seldom hit the ball right where we want it. On particularly high balls, move well behind the bounce about five to six feet and wait for the ball to drop into your strike zone. On low shots, again position yourself behind the ball and bend your knees so that you can make contact as close to your strike zone as possible.

Rotate your body

Once you're in position, watch the ball bounce and rise. As it moves into your strike zone, step forward and rotate your shoulders and hips toward the ball. Let that rotation move your racket and, just before you strike the ball, squeeze the bottom three fingers of your racket hand. This will keep your grip strong, your wrist firm and your racket head stable.

The key to controlling your shots lies in controlling the face of your racket. When all is said and done, the ball will go where your strings are pointing at impact. Its pace will be determined by the speed of your racket head and spin will come from the path of your swing. So, as you make contact with the ball, be sure to position your racket face so that your strings are pointing toward your target.

The next time you take the court, try this little timing exercise: When you see the ball land on your side of the court, say "bounce" to yourself. Watch it rise toward its peak and move into your strike zone. Now rotate your body and, as you feel your strings make contact with the ball, say "hit." This is a great technique for developing both your ball watching skills and timing

When a photographer takes a picture, he holds the camera still for a split second after he's snapped the shot. Do the same every time you hit the tennis ball. Keep your head focused on your contact point for a brief moment after you've struck the ball. This will help ensure that your body stays balanced and, in turn, your racket head remains under control.

The stroke doesn't end at contact

After you've struck the ball, continue rotating forward until your racket's pointing at your target. Some players make the mistake of stopping their swing as soon as they make contact with the ball, or immediately wrapping their racket around their necks. Both can lead to mis-hits and loss of control, as well as putting a tremendous amount of stress on a player's arms.

A long follow-through provides your racket with a path to follow and encourages you to hit completely through the ball. Your racket head stays in a fixed position for an extended period of time, which means that if you mis-time your shot or get a bad bounce, you'll still have a pretty good chance of making solid contact and maintaining your control.

To help develop a long follow-through, imagine swinging through three balls, one right after the other. After you make contact with the ball, keep rotating forward as if you had to hit another ball, and yet another one on the same path. Keep your racket moving forward until it is pointing toward your target.

Keep your strokes simple and you'll be amazed at how consistent and accurate your shots will become. My

Strike Zone

wife is a perfect example of this approach. Kelley was one of the country's top junior players throughout much of the 70s. When hitting her groundstrokes, she brings her racket relatively straight back and swings low to high, with a firm wrist. No exaggerated grip, huge looping swing or new age stance. Kelley has superb footwork, catches virtually every ball in her strike zone and finishes pointing toward her target.

She has a very basic stroke, but has superb timing and control of her racket head. As a result, she hits more consistently, more accurately and, for my power-obsessed readers, harder than most men.

Read, ready, run and rotate. Focus on the four R's and you'll immediately hit the ball better. I guarantee it!

Chapter 3

Three Secrets To Defeat Stinky Feet

G reg, you have nice strokes but your feet stink," barked my old college coach, Norm Copeland, at the end of my very first varsity practice.

After thinking for a few minutes and a quick check of my feet, I realized that Norm was not referring to the aroma coming from my tennis shoes but rather their lack of movement.

Tennis is usually thought of as a game of strokes, but Norm knew that it is a game of steps, and what you do with those steps will more often than not determine the quality of your shot.

While sound stroking mechanics are certainly important, what good are they if you can't get into position to execute them? Once you have a firm grasp of the game's basic techniques, you must next develop your footwork. Good footwork usually equals proper positioning, which then allows you to execute a smooth and controlled stroke.

No shot in tennis should be hit behind, or on top of, your body. That being the case, you should always position yourself far enough in back of, and to the side of, the

> *Footwork is the most important part of the game. It's everything.*
>
> Brad Gilbert
> Former touring pro and coach of
> Andre Agassi and Andy Roddick

ball so that when the time comes to swing you have to take a step forward and slightly reach to the side to hit.

When hitting from this position, your body's rotation and weight transfer provide the power as well as absorb the shock of hitting the ball.   When you're out of position, your elbow, wrist and shoulder have to provide the juice and absorb the shock. That's one of the main reasons why so many recreational players have tennis elbow.   Their arms are working too hard to compensate for poor positioning.

Proper positioning is vital to sound strokes, and the positioning process begins before your opponent has even struck their shot. It begins with your ready position.

Are you really "ready"?

Many players, when waiting for their opponent's shot, adopt what I call the "waiting-in- line-at-the-movies" ready position. They stand perfectly still, arms dangling at their sides and their heels flat on the ground. While these players may be prepared to view the latest blockbuster, they are not ready to react quickly to a well-hit tennis ball.

When your feet are firmly planted on the ground, it's as if your entire body weight is trying to push you down through the floor. If you weigh 180 pounds and are standing still, imagine having a 180-pound weight on top of your head. When your opponent hits his shot, your first movement won't be to react toward the ball, but rather to push that weight off your head so you can begin to move.

The high-tech term for this is "unweighting." With less than two seconds to react, get into position and execute your shot, having to "unweight" your body wastes valuable time. Instead, I want you to use an active ready position.

Stand with both hands holding the racket out in front of your body. Your knees should be shoulder-width apart and slightly bent. Stay up on your toes and keep your feet moving, either side-to-side or bouncing up and down. This may be familiar advice but its advice that cannot be repeated enough.

Take a strong split step

Just before your opponent's racket makes contact with the ball, you must execute what is, without question, one of the most important elements in the game—the split step. This is a small hop, about two to three inches off the ground, timed so that you are in the air as your opponent strikes the ball. While in the air, you'll see where your opponent's shot is going and can begin your preparation.

Geoff Norton, one of the world's top teaching professionals has his students actually say the word "split" out loud, at the appropriate time, to remind themselves to split step before every shot their opponents hit. All—I repeat, all—good players split step before every shot!

As you land, whether at the baseline or up at net, be sure to keep your feet one to two feet apart so that you can immediately spring off your toes. Turn your shoulders and hips towards the ball while preparing your racket at the same time. Move toward the ball as quickly as possible. As you approach your hitting position, roughly five feet behind the ball's bounce, make your steps shorter and more frequent.

These short steps will not only help you fine-tune your position, they'll also keep your body in balance. Being balanced allows you to execute your stroke as well as make any last-second adjustments in the event that you get a bad bounce or misjudge the ball

To test your balance after you complete your follow-through, try to hold your finishing position. If you can, without moving your feet, you've executed a balanced stroke.

There's an excellent product on the market called the Ultimate Balance Trainer (More info: ultimatebalance.com). It's a small device that you attach to your hat or visor. As you move around the court, the device tells you if your body is leaning too far forward or back, or if it's drifting to the left or right. You actually hear a little voice say to you, "left," "right," "front," or "back." It's a great tool to help you work on your balance.

Remember the ball does come back

The moment you've finished your shot, begin to shuffle back toward the center of the court. Keep your feet moving and, again, split step just before your opponent hits his next shot. Think of each point as one continuous movement, not a series of stops and starts. The average point in tennis lasts between three to six seconds and the only time your feet should be still is when you're striking the ball.

Behind every solid stroke is great footwork. Work on improving your movement around the court and you'll soon find that, as your footwork improves, your strokes will miraculously become easier to execute. Here's a drill Coach Copeland gave me that I still use today.

Service Box Drill

Start in the center of the service box facing the net. Shuffle as quickly as possible to your right and, using a cross-over step, touch the singles sideline with your front foot and simulate hitting a low volley, making sure to bend your knees so that your back knee is as close to the ground as possible. Recover back to the center of the box, then repeat to your left. Do this, alternating between right and left, 10 times, then take a one-minute rest. Do three to five sets of this drill and increase the repetitions as your stamina improves.

Keep them moving!

Split-Step

A FUNNY FOOTWORK FABLE

Jenny was a very wealthy lady who had grown accustomed to being served. She stayed in the best hotels, ate at the finest restaurants and only traveled first class.

Jenny also loved to hit tennis balls. The only problem was that she didn't like to run. As with her life off the court, Jenny felt that the ball should be brought to her to hit. This, combined with the fact that she was a bit on the heavy side, made movement a constant issue during our lessons.

Jenny had a great sense of humor and we often joked about her lack of interest in running for the ball. I would hit to her so that the most she would have to move would be a step or two. Anything farther than that was out of the question.

If I did happen to hit one out of her immediate reach, she'd give me a mock offended look and say, "Now Greg, you know I'm not going to run for that one." It became a running (or lack thereof) joke.

One day Jenny came to my court and even the one step to the left or right was too much to ask. After watching Jenny stand still for nine shots in a row, I gave her my own offended look and said, "For God's sake, Jenny, do you want me to come over there and hit it for you, too?"

Jenny paused, thought for a second, and with a mischievous look in her eye, smiled and said, "How much extra would that cost?"

Chapter 4

Your Roadmap To The Next Level

Another summer has ended, exactly the same way as the previous three—a straight-set loss in the first round of the club championships.

This was going to be your breakthrough year. No more silly unforced errors, lapses in concentration or third-set fatigue. You took the court against Bobby, a player you beat regularly. You confidently popped the top off a fresh can of balls and began your road to the trophy.

One hour later, you walked off court a straight-set loser, and all you had to show for your efforts were a sore arm, a can of used balls and a "good match" comment from Bobby. To make matters worse, you know what Bobby really meant to say was, "Ha! I've been playing two years less than you, and I won."

Needless to say, you're fuming. You go through the usual list of excuses that creep into everyone's mind immediately after a bad loss: "The sun was in my eyes, my racket was strung too loose, he cheated, my pro stinks," blah, blah, blah.

While these rationalizations may make you feel better temporarily, by the time you've showered, reclaimed your rackets from the trash can and settled into your car for the ride home, you force yourself to face a disturbing fact. In the past three years your game has not improved one bit. You still can't keep the ball in play consistently, your backhand stinks and God forbid you miss your first serve, because your second serve. . .well, enough said.

We've all gone through periods of frustration when we've felt that our games are struck in neutral. Tennis is a sneaky game, because improvement can initially come quickly. In many cases, someone who has just picked up a racket and had a few lessons can rally back and forth a bit, pop in 50 percent of his serves and begin playing the game.

This "instant improvement" is seductive, yet it is also deceptive. New players often feel that they'll continually improve at this rate, and within six months they'll be clearing space on their mantle for their trophies. While progress may come quickly at first, in order to move to the higher levels of the game, you need to do more than come to the courts once or twice a week and play a few casual sets.

That being the case, I'm happy to say that with a little effort and a good plan, it's possible for every player to improve. Here are some time-proven methods that are sure to help you climb the next rung on the way to reaching your potential.

Take a hard look at your game

What do you do well? What do you do poorly? If you lost ten pounds, would you move around the court better? I've included a very brief self-evaluation in Appendix B, which focuses on the major areas of the game. Don't worry, it's short and straight to the point. It should take you all of three minutes to complete. I've filled one out below as an example.

Write a sentence or two in each section dealing with your strengths and weaknesses. Be honest with yourself and focus on both your physical and mental games. Simply thinking about your game and jotting down a few notes is the first step toward making you a better player. Take the time to do it!

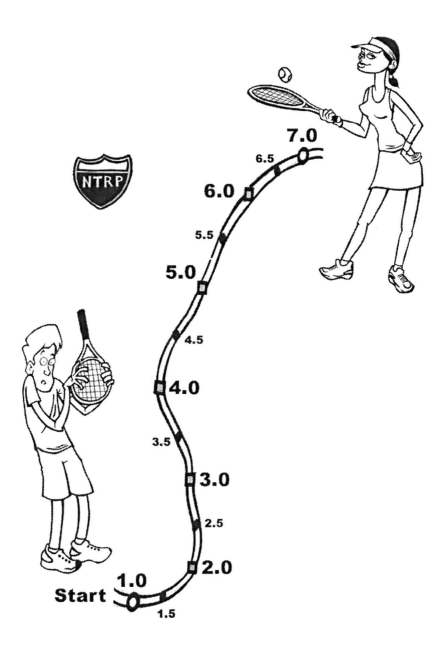

Your roadmap to the next level.

TENNIS SKILLS INVENTORY
Name: *Greg Moran*

Write a few brief sentences in each section. This is for
your own benefit, so you can see which areas you need to
work on.

Table 4-1

Forehand	*Inconsistent and frequently late. I need to work on staying away from the ball.*
Backhand	*Slice is good but topspin needs a lot of work.*
Volleys	*Forehand volley is solid but backhand volley collapses under pressure.*
Overhead	*Consistent but need to remind myself to keep my head up on contact.*
Serve	*Slice is my best serve. Topspin needs work, as does my placement.*
Return of serve	*Need to move forward into the ball more.*
Fitness: strength, agility, endurance and flexibility.	*Agility, strength and endurance are good.* *Flexibility needs work.*
Mental game: Ability to concentrate, control temper, fight back when playing poorly or when behind, ability to put forth a consistent effort both in practice and play.	*Mind wanders frequently. Am usually able to keep my temper in check. Effort in practice could be greater.*

If you feel comfortable doing so, ask one of your playing
partners to assess your game. Most players love to talk
about tennis and will be happy to give you their
thoughts—some even without you asking. This will give

you a good idea of where you are and what you need to do to get where you want to go.

You don't play tennis to get in shape. You get in shape to play tennis

While sound strokes are certainly important, they're of little use if you can't get into position or don't have the energy to execute them. It's very tough to get back for a deep overhead if you're carrying an extra 15 pounds of pizza and ice cream around your waist.

As your game improves, so must your level of fitness. Points and matches become longer and more strenuous and simply playing the game a few times a week won't be enough to keep you in top shape. By doing additional off-court exercises you'll be able to keep up with the demands that your improving play requires, as well as lessen the chance you'll suffer an injury that could keep you off the courts for an extended period of time.

When I suggest to my students that they do off-court training, the juniors generally look at me as if I'm out of my mind and the adults simply say, "This is my exercise, and I'm lucky to find the time for tennis, let alone off-court exercises." Sorry, but I don't buy it.

Granted, we live in an over-scheduled society where most of us seem forever pressed for time. However, if you're interested in improving the level of your tennis, not to mention the quality of your life, you need to make the time. Get up half an hour early, watch a little less television or take a shorter lunch break. We're all busy, but what's more important than your health?

Space-Age Fitness

If you think tennis has become high-tech, the fitness industry makes it look prehistoric. Walk into any fitness center in the country and you'll feel as if you've entered a NASA space station.

> *If you don't take care of your body, where will you live?*
>
> Anonymous

There are odd-looking, computerized machines designed to work every part of your body. We're told that they'll give us arms like Arnold and abs like Anna Kournikova. They're very stylish, with bright colors and fluorescent lights. Some even talk to you, telling you if you're going too fast or too slow, how many reps you've done or how many laps you have to go. I once even had a machine scold me for leaving it sweaty after I got off it.

For the layperson, fitness has become as confusing as quantum mechanics, yet the question remains: "What should I do, and how often should I do it?" Sammy Samson, a former World Natural Bodybuilding Champion and personal trainer to numerous celebrities and professional athletes says, "You don't need to belong to a high-tech gym or do a ridiculous amount of exercise to improve your tennis and your health. Simply adding a few off-court activities to your regular tennis workout will make you feel fitter physically and psychologically, both on the court and off."

Sammy says to focus on these key areas:

1. Endurance
2. Agility
3. Flexibility & Strength

Endurance

A tennis match consists of anywhere between 300-500 short sprints. To prepare for that, you need something for your heart that will simulate these short bursts of speed. Jogging is fine, though you may find it hard on your joints, particularly if you're on the older side of 30. Swimming and biking are also great.

Whichever activity you choose, be sure to mix in short sprints. For example, jog for one minute and then sprint for 10 seconds before resuming your jog. Bike for one minute, then sprint for 15 seconds. Swim one lap slowly, and sprint the next. This mirrors the work that your heart has to do on the tennis court.

Agility

To this day, I have not found a better agility exercise than jumping rope. It's a great cardiovascular workout and also strengthens your muscles. You can jump rope virtually anywhere and a plastic beaded rope costs as little as a three dollars.

If your knees are a little tender, stay off hard surfaces and jump on a cushioned or carpeted floor.

Begin slowly and start off jumping using both feet. Move the rope with your wrists, jump only three to four inches off the ground and land on the balls of your feet. Here is a simple jump-rope program to get you started.

Both feet:	10 times
Right foot:	10 times
Left foot:	10 times
Alternating feet:	10 times

Slowly increase your numbers as your technique and fitness improve.

Another excellent agility exercise is racket jumps. Place your racket on the ground and stand on the right side of the racket, next to the grip. With your feet approximately 12 inches apart, jump sideways over the grip and back again. Repeat this 20 times and then take a breather. Next, place the racket in front of you and jump forward and back over the grip 20 times. Build up your stamina so that you can either increase the number of sets or the repetitions per set for each exercise. Be sure to stretch your calves after these exercises.

Climb off the treadmill and take a Cardio Tennis class

There's a new fitness activity in town and it's called Cardio Tennis. Conducted on a tennis court by certified tennis professionals, each class consists of a short warm-up, a cardio workout in which you're moving and constantly hitting tennis balls, and a cool down phase.

With upbeat music playing in the background, Cardio Tennis is a great workout, lots and fun and will improve both your endurance and agility. (More info: Cardio Tennis classes in your area can be found at cardiotennis.com.)

Flexibility & Strength

Several years ago, one of my students gave me a one-hour private yoga lesson. The weightlifter in me said that yoga was for "wimps," but I was able to push that ignoramus aside and give it a shot. Sixty minutes later, my thoughts on fitness had changed forever. Yoga workouts have significantly improved my balance, strength and flexibility. I'm also more relaxed, better able to focus and suffer far fewer injuries.

Yoga, like tennis, can be practiced at any age, from 4 to 104, and today there are more than 15 million people doing it in the United States alone! It's inexpensive, can be done anywhere and by anyone. Maria Sharapova, Serena Williams and John McEnroe are among those who have climbed onto the yoga mat as part of their training program.

I've found that Ashtanga yoga provides the most complete combination of strength, flexibility and stamina (More info: yoga.com).

A word of caution: Like any form of exercise, some yoga poses can be quite difficult and should not be attempted without a qualified teacher. I suggest attending a yoga class in your area conducted by a certified instructor to get the proper start.

Find a good pro and take some lessons

The Great Big Bill Tilden never had a tennis lesson. However, for most of us, it's easier with a little help along the way. A few sessions with a great teaching professional can go a long way toward jumpstarting your game.

When searching for an instructor, look for one who is accredited by either of the two primary teaching organizations—the Professional Tennis Registry (More info: ptrtennis.org) or the United States Professional Tennis Association (More info: uspta.org).

In order to attain certification by either of these organizations, a candidate must pass stringent on and off-court tests that cover all aspects of playing and teaching the game, as well as the business side of the industry. If a pro has one of these certifications—some have both—you can be relatively certain that they know their stuff. Go to the organizations' websites and you can find a certified professional in your area.

When you meet your pro for the first time, he'll undoubtedly ask you two key questions: "What are your tennis goals?" and "How often are you able to play?"

Show him your self-evaluation, tell him about your goals and how much time you can devote to improving. For some tennis players, the goal is to win more matches, while others simply want to get some exercise and learn to play well enough to enjoy tennis with their spouses.

After a lesson or two, the pro will have a good feel for your ability as well as your mental approach to the game. He'll also have thoughts on what you need to change and add to your game to improve. At that point, the two of you can sit down and come up with a game plan for improvement. This plan will include both short- and long-term goals.   Short-term goals might be things like changing a grip, adding a new shot or getting fitter. Your short-term goals should lead to a long-term goal such as team tryouts or a big match. As you conquer each of your short-term goals, you'll get an injection of enthusiasm as you see your game improving.

Every month or so, sit down with your pro and evaluate your progress. Cross off the small goals you've attained and add new ones as you make your way to your larger goal: making the school or club team or performing well in the big tournament. (More info: Appendix C. Goals Program Worksheet).

Tennis lessons are not cheap, so each time you walk onto the court, have a specific idea of what you'd like to focus on. Ask questions and take advantage of the pro's knowledge. Otherwise, you may wind up working on a little bit of everything and not enough of anything.

Don't "play," practice

How many times per week do you practice your tennis skills? I don't mean walking onto the court, hitting a few shots and then saying, "Serve 'em up." Practice means stepping onto the court with a specific plan to maximize your time and working on various aspects of your game.

So I'll ask you again, "How many times a week do you practice?" For many players, the answer is zero.

Unless you're a professional, tennis is not the top priority in your life, nor should it be. If you're a junior player, there's school, other activities and your social life, all competing for your time. If you're an adult, the pressures on you are even greater. The time you can set aside for tennis is at a premium, so when you do step onto the court, you want to hit as many balls as possible. Playing sets and matches seldom accomplishes this because the ball is generally in play for a short period of time.

Find another player who likes to "practice" and whose goals and ability are similar to yours. At least once a week, walk on the court with a specific plan and a set of drills that will allow you to hit as many balls as possible, which is always more fun, and work on your game.

When you walk on the court to practice, do so with the same focus and intensity that you would if you were playing a tournament final. Chase down and hit every ball with energy and purpose.

Jimmy Connors was well known for his relatively brief yet incredibly intense practice sessions. Joel Drucker, author of the captivating book Jimmy Connors Saved My Life says, "When Connors practiced, the emphasis was on quality over quantity. That meant going for every ball on one bounce, playing balls that were out of the court, constantly moving his feet.

You would never, ever see Connors stop in the middle of a rally, pick up a ball that bounced past the baseline and start the rally again. Instead, he'd play balls from all corners, always moving. Rarely was he on-court longer than 90 minutes at a time. Rather than leave a court tired, he left it eager."

Try a heart rate monitor

I've recently begun to wear a heart rate monitor when I work out and have found that it works wonders as far as motivating me to keep up the intensity. The monitor, which fits around your chest, will measure the intensity of your workout and give you a reading on a special watch you wear on your wrist. They give exact measurements and can tell you whether to pick it up or slow it down. It's like having a personal trainer on the court with you. Polar (More info: polarusa.com) makes the best that I've seen.

My favorite practice partner

I've been fortunate in that, for the past 23 years, I've been married to my favorite practice partner. As I mentioned, my wife Kelley is a heck of a tennis player. We first laid eyes on each other at the tennis courts at Rollins College where Kelley was a star on the women's team, and I was happy just to be on the men's team.

We had a class together, ironically called "The Family," and soon after began practicing together. Twenty-five years, two children and a mortgage later, we still love to get out on the court together and work out. In fact, many have joked over the years that the reason we got married was that we would always have someone to play with. Actually, that's only partially true.

Musicians practice their scales, doctors operate on hundreds of cadavers before they perform surgery on a living patient, and you need to hit thousands of crosscourt forehands in drills before you gain the confidence to pass your archrival with it in the club championships.

Here is a sample one-hour practice program that will take you through all aspects of your game. Be sure to:

- Warm-up before taking the court: Jump rope, do jumping jacks, run in place, anything to break a light sweat. Don't waste precious court time getting loose.
- Take a basket or several cans of balls to the court: This will minimize pick-up time.
- Practice with the same intensity and enthusiasm with which you play a match.

One-Hour Practice Routine

1. Mini-tennis, inside the service lines. 3 minutes
2. Full-court rally, lengthening your strokes. 3 minutes
3. Crosscourt forehands. 5 minutes
4. Crosscourt backhands. 5 minutes
5. Down-the-line forehands. 5 minutes
6. Down-the-line backhands. 5 minutes
7. Rally for depth: Hit beyond the service line. 5 minutes
8. Reflex volleys from service lines. 4 minutes
9. Groundstroke/volley: One player at the net, the other at the baseline. Switch after 5 minutes.
10. Overheads/lobs: Player at the baseline hits only lobs; player at the net returns overheads. Switch after 5 minutes.
11. Serve and return: One player serves, the other returns away from the server. Switch after 2 1/2 minutes.

Take this plan to the court and adjust the time to suit your needs. If, in your last match, you served great but your forehand gave you fits, spend additional time on your forehand and cut out the serving.

Many players say that they find practicing boring but, believe me, it's not nearly as boring as playing the same mediocre tennis year after year.

What if I don't have anyone to practice with?

No problem. Track down a backboard. Bjorn Borg used one when he was learning the game and Jimmy Connors still uses one today. A backboard can be one of your most effective practice partners. It always wants to play, doesn't get tired and never misses.

When I was a junior player, I once spent an entire winter playing in a program and never once stepped onto a tennis court. The program was conducted by Brian Eisner, the legendary former coach of the University of Michigan men's team, and was held in a gymnasium.

Eisner had different stations set up and we would practice hitting into various size squares of adhesive tape. Each week we were able to practice every stroke, refine our consistency and accuracy and hit thousands of balls.

Most clubs and public parks have a backboard. If you can't find one, try your local school or YMCA. They'll usually let you use their gym. Here's a 60-minute backboard program.

Take approximately 10 steps from the wall. This should place you approximately 21 feet from the wall, the distance from the net to the service line.

One Hour Backboard Program

1. Hit forehands gently against the wall. Pick a specific spot or tape up a square to use as a target. Take short swings and let the ball bounce once. Try to keep it going as many times as you can. 5 minutes.

2. Switch to backhand. 5 minutes
3. Then alternate between forehand and backhand. 5 minutes
4. Take nine more steps away from the backboard. This will put you approximately 39 feet from the wall, the distance from the net to the baseline. Repeat step one. Increase the size of your swing to hit a full groundstroke. Forehands 5 minutes
5. Backhands 5 minutes
6. Alternate between forehand and backhand. 5 minutes
7. Take 15 steps forward, which should place you about nine feet from the wall. Practice your volleys, using a short, compact motion. Forehand volley 5 minutes
8. Backhand volley 5 minutes
9. Alternate between forehand and backhand volley. 5 minutes
10. Practice overheads by hitting the ball off the ground close to the wall, so that it bounces high in the air off the backboard. 5 minutes
11. For the next 5 minutes, move from one area to the other, starting at the baseline distance from the wall. Hit five forehands, then five backhands. Then move to the service line spot and hit volleys, five of each. Finally move to the net position and hit five forehand volleys, then five backhand volleys, without letting the ball bounce. Try to complete the entire cycle without missing
12. Serve for 5 minutes. Aim for various spots on the wall.

Keep a tennis journal

Buy a three-ring binder and begin to put together a tennis journal. Take notes on your lessons, plan out your practice and workout sessions, and jot down thoughts and questions that come to mind as you play or practice. Put together scouting reports on players that you have faced or that you are likely to come up against in the future. You can also keep in your journal interesting and informative articles you come across.

There are many ready-made tennis journals on the market. The best one I've seen is called The Tennis Workbook and was put together by Jody Belsher. It's 98 pages long and can be kept in your tennis bag.

The Tennis Workbook (More info: tennisworkbook.com) has tabbed sections for easy access and contains a self-evaluation, a phone directory, a place to record match results, a tournament planner and a variety of tennis tips. The book is well worth the $14.95 cost.

You can also put together your own journal. I have two—one for playing and one for teaching.

> A notebook should be an integral part of your equipment. So many things pop up that if you record your learning process in diary form, you'll be amazed at how much valuable information you will gather.
>
> Arthur Ashe
> Three-time Grand Slam singles champion

In my teaching journal, I keep notes on all my students. I have their contact information, what we've worked on in lessons, their goals and my plans for their next lesson. I also have hundreds of articles that I've collected over the years that I've found interesting and that have helped me in my teaching.

In my playing journal, I keep information that helps me with my game: practice routines, notes, articles or quotes, fitness workouts, contact information for practice partners and tournament schedules.

Buy a journal or design your own. It doesn't really matter as long as you begin to put your thoughts and goals down on paper. Again, the more planning and thought you give to your game, the faster you'll improve.

Study the game

By reading books and watching videos by the experts you'll deepen your understanding of the techniques and strategies that make a winning tennis player. You'll also learn about the game's fascinating history and issues. You'll find anything by Vic Braden, Dennis Van der Meer, Peter Burwash, Paul Fein, Joel Drucker and Peter Bodo to be both interesting and educational.

Give yourself something to look forward to

Seeing the same face across the same net at the same club week after week, month after month can begin to feel like eating stale bread. Mix it up and schedule a few special days throughout the month. It could be a tournament, a match with a new player, a tennis vacation, or simply a game at a different club—anything that gets you out of your tennis routine and keeps you pumped up about the game.

There's no shortcut to improvement

The amount of time you devote to your game will determine your rate of progress. Establish realistic expectations based on how much of yourself you can give to tennis. If once a week is all you can manage, enjoy the hour, get some exercise, laugh a lot and pat yourself on the back for getting out there.

Twice a week is great. In fact, the biggest difference I see is when players move from playing once to twice a week. With this frequency, it's reasonable to expect some consistency in your game. You should even see improvement over time.

Three times a week is ideal if you can manage it. If you can make one of your outings some form of instruction, another a practice session and the third a match, you've got it all covered.

During the lesson you can work on your techniques and learn new shots. In practice, you can groove your shots, and in a match you can incorporate them into a game plan. On this schedule you should see consistent improvement over time.

Above all, don't burden yourself with a timetable for progress. It'll stress you out, slow down your progress and take away the fun of the process. Sandy is a 48-year-old single parent with a thriving medical practice. He schedules an hour lesson once a week with me and keeps the appointment about a quarter of the time. Last week, after about 15 minutes of extremely erratic hitting, Sandy threw his racket in disgust.

I brought him up to the net and asked him, *"When was the last time you played?"*

"Last week," he replied.

"No," I reminded him, *"you had to cancel that one because one of your kids got sick."*

"OK, it was the week before," he said.

"No, you had an emergency at the office. Remember?"

Sandy soon realized that the last time he held a racket in his hand was a month ago. I reassured him by telling him that he was "the best once-a-month player at the club." He laughed and then went back to the baseline and enjoyed the rest of his lesson.

When you get in the car to drive cross-country you map out a route. Do the same with your tennis.

Take a few minutes to evaluate your game. Spend some time with a pro and hit the practice courts with a specific program and you'll be well on your way to reaching your potential.

> *"Don't look for the big, quick improvement; seek the small improvement, one day at a time. That's the only way it happens, and when it happens, it lasts."*
>
> John Wooden
> Legendary basketball coach

Part 2

Retro Shots That Will Raise Your Game

Hundreds of books have been written on the various theories regarding tennis strokes. They're talked about on the courts, discussed in the gym and are even a source of cocktail party conversation.

The other day, while in a restaurant, I overheard one man saying to another with more than a little bit of condescension in his voice, "My pro has me working on the open-stance forehand with a full-Western grip. He feels that this, combined with my improved dynamic balance and better use of my kinetic chain will definitely bring me to the next level." I wanted to enlist my kinetic chain and smack the guy.

I've always felt that gripping and swinging the tennis racket should be simple and instinctive, not complicated and mechanical. Patrick McEnroe, captain of the United States Davis Cup team, says "strokes are like fingerprints—no two are exactly alike."

I said in the Introduction to this book that I won't be advocating any major grip or stroking changes to improve your tennis, and I meant it. However, I do think it's important for your education as a tennis player to know the various grips used in the game and to understand their advantages and disadvantages.

In Appendix D you'll find an easy-to-read chart that describes the five main grips of the game as well as a few of their advantages and disadvantages. As you move along, don't be afraid to experiment a bit with some different grips. Have some fun with them.

There are three—and only three—stroking techniques you need to concern yourself with: groundstrokes, volleys, and serves. That's it. Yes, I know, there are far more than three shots in the game. But all shots, in some way or another, are born from one of these three techniques. Develop a feel for these and you're well on your way to developing the strokes that make up a winning tennis player's game.

Unless otherwise noted, all technical instruction is from a right-handed player's perspective.

Chapter 5

One Shot
To The Next Level

Your mouth is undoubtedly watering as you wonder which shot will immediately take your tennis to the next level. Is it the forehand? The volley? Maybe it's the overhead smash? I'll give you a little hint: it's the shot that starts every single point.

That's right. The serve is the most important shot in the game of tennis because it is the first shot hit and often sets the tone for the entire point. If you can make your serve a weapon, you'll be able to compete with any player at the club.

I've always found it interesting that players are eager to practice their groundstrokes and net game, yet frequently shy away from working on their serve. As a result, their serve is often a level or two below the rest of their game. This imbalance eventually catches up with them when they attempt to play in upper level leagues or tournaments against accomplished players.

One of my students, James, is an intermediate player but has developed an advanced player's serve. We play every Saturday morning at 6:30, and James always gets to the club 20 minutes early to practice his serve. As a result, his serve is actually a level above the rest of his game and allows him to hold his own in matches with people who, for the most part, are stronger players

The serve is the one shot in the game that puts you totally in control. You can take your time to hit it and don't have to react to something your opponent has hit to you. That being the case, your serve should become your biggest weapon.

It begins with the toss

When you develop control over your toss, you'll automatically move your serve to the next level. A well-placed toss allows you to swing your racket smoothly and transfer your body weight into the ball.

How's your toss? Let's find out. Grab your racket and a ball and go through your service motion, toss the ball and let it drop to the ground. Make a mark, or place a coin, on the spot where the ball lands. Repeat this five times, each time marking the spot where the ball lands. Now, swing your arm in the service motion and stop it in front of your body, at your point of contact.

Slowly drop your arm until your racket head touches the court. This will show you roughly where your service toss should have landed. How many of your tossing marks are in the right spot?

If you're struggling to control your toss while trying to do the classic "down-together-up-together" service motion, start with your racket in the back-scratch position. This will allow you to focus solely on your tossing arm.

Here are two quick tips to help you groove your toss:

1. Imagine balancing a glass of water in the palm of your hand as you release the ball. This will help you place the ball out in front of your body.

2. Try to toss the ball in the air without it spinning. This will help you cut down on any wrist flick or finger roll that can throw your toss off course.

Remember, successful tennis strokes are a function of positioning, and the positioning aspect of your serve is the toss. A properly placed toss will allow you to swing your racket smoothly. This will help you hit a consistent serve that you can control and add pace to when you like.

Throw a touchdown pass

Your service motion should mirror that of a quarterback throwing a 50-yard pass: up and out with a wrist snap at contact. Remember this mantra when serving: swing up, snap down.

I once had a student who, without a doubt, had the worst service motion in the history of tennis. Her arm went every which way, and she ended up flicking her racket at the ball using her elbow and wrist. To call it "ugly" would be kind!

After showing her that the proper service motion was like throwing a football, I told her to take 50 practice throws a day. She took the tip to heart and each day practiced throwing a rolled up pair of socks against a wall in her bedroom 150 times! She developed a service motion that was the envy of every player at the club—myself included!

Another great exercise to practice your serve is to hold a tennis ball in each hand and go through your service motion. After you've tossed the first ball, watch it reach its peak and then throw the second ball and try to hit your toss. This allows you to practice both your toss and swing. You can even do this one in the comfort of your home. Just replace the tennis balls with socks.

Make your serve a weapon

Boom or bust. This is the way many players approach their serve. They launch a rocket on their first serve, hoping that, if it goes in, they'll get an easy point as well as intimidate their opponent with their "awesome" power. It's a freebie in their minds because they know that if it doesn't go in they can always "plop" in their second serve and still be in the point.

While this is not necessarily a bad strategy with the weekend wannabes who don't have the skills to take advantage of a powder puff second serve, a strong player will eat that "plop" second serve for lunch

There's much more to a strong serve than merely trying to overpower your opponent. Sure, big serves are nice but service winners for most players are few and far between. A better approach is to view your serve as a tool to gain control of the point. You do this by first getting it in on a consistent basis while also keeping your opponent guessing as to where you're going to hit it.

Players with strong serves have learned to get a high percentage of their first serves in and actually swing just as hard, sometimes harder, on their second. Their secret lies in the use of spin.

Become a spin master

Spin is nature's gift to tennis. It enhances both our consistency and control, and by learning to put slice and topspin on your serve you'll keep your opponent scrambling, right from the start of the point.

Spin serves are best hit with the Continental grip. This grip puts the racket at an angle in your hand, which, depending upon how you swing your arm and snap your wrist, allows you to make the ball dance.

When a right-handed player hits a serve with heavy slice, imagining the ball as the face of a clock, make contact at 3:00 and swing around as if

> *"You're only as good as your second serve."*
>
> Peter Burwash
> Internationally renowned
> teaching professional

you're peeling an orange. The ball will hit the court and kick severely to the receiver's right.

A serve hit with severe topspin (swinging up and out from 7:00-1:00 on the clock) will clear the net by a large margin, making it a "safe" serve, and then kick up in the receivers face. Both spins will force your opponent to hit the ball out of their strike zone and will often result in an error or weak return, which you can then attack.

Placement is always more important than power

By moving your serve around to different areas of the service box, you'll keep your opponent guessing. The next time you go to the practice court try this exercise: Take twelve tennis balls, put one on top of three, making three small towers. Place one in each corner of the service box and the last one in the middle.

Next, take a basket of balls and start aiming for the towers, one at a time. Tell yourself that you're going to stay out there until you knock over all of the towers. You'll probably be out there for quite a while, but if you do this a few times a week, I guarantee you'll develop an accurate serve.

You can also keep your opponent off balance by varying where you stand along the baseline. Pick a spot close to the centerline, another mid way between the centerline and sideline and a third close to the sideline. When you serve from these three points, it will change the angle of your serve as it moves toward your opponent, making it more awkward to return.

If you can hit your topspin and slice serves to all three areas of the service box, from three different spots along the baseline, you'll have eighteen different serves to throw at your opponent. If you can throw in the occasional flat serve to all three spots, from all three

"I missed my big hard first serve again. Now I have to get this one in."

areas of the baseline, you'll have 27 different serves at your disposal. That's quite an arsenal!

Develop a serving ritual

Each time you step up to the line to serve, you need to relax and clear your head. This is best done by developing a serving ritual. It can be a series of movements such as bouncing the ball a certain number of times, adjusting your hat ala Jim Courier or taking several deep breaths. Here's Maria Sharapova's serving ritual:

1. Adjusts her strings
2. Touches her hair twice
3. Takes a deep breath
4. Bounces the ball twice

Develop a personal ritual to go through before every serve. If you're nervous, go through it twice. It will help to put your mind and body in sync and allow you to focus on hitting your best serve.

There is no excuse for not having a strong serve. Take to the court with a big basket of balls and work on:

1. Developing a consistent toss and motion
2. Learning the Continental grip
3. Developing the slice and topspin serves
4. Placing your serve to different areas of the court.
5. Developing a serving ritual

Be sure to practice all of your serves from both sides of the court as well as from different spots along the baseline. Developing your serve can be a lonely, sometimes boring proposition. However, I can assure you that the type of game an effective serve allows you to play is anything but boring.

Chapter 6

Who's Afraid Of The Big Bad Server?

Players with big serves are used to intimidating their opponents with their power, but nothing takes the wind out of their sails faster than an opponent who shows no fear and can spit their big serve right back at them. With that in mind, your top priority when returning serve is to get every ball back in play. After that, you want to minimize, if not neutralize, the server's advantage.

Getting ready

Below are the approximate times you have to react to your opponent's serve based on its speed.

Speed of serve (mph)	Reaction time (seconds)
90	.59
80	.66
70	.76
60	.88
50	1.06

If you find yourself across the net from Andy Roddick and Andy fires in one of his 140-mph bombs, you'll have less than half a second to react and respond. Fortunately, we don't have to face supersonic serves very often. Players rated at the 2.0 to 4.0 levels generally serve in the 40- to 60-mph range. Players at the 4.0-4.5 level and above can often get it up into the 80s, which gives you a little over half a second to execute your return (More info: Appendix

A. Ratings). That's still not a lot of time, but with proper positioning before the serve, as well as an active ready position, you can make your return of serve a weapon.

Where to stand

As you wait for your opponent to serve, line up as close to (or inside of) the baseline as possible and a foot or two inside the singles sideline. This will allow you to return the ball back to the server quickly as well as position yourself to cover both sides equally.

As the server prepares to toss the ball, move into your active ready position and have an idea of what you want to do with your return based on your opponent's style of play. Follow these general guidelines for both singles and doubles:

1. If your opponent serves and stays back, aim at least 2-3 feet over the net and return deep and crosscourt.

2. If you're facing a serve and volley opponent, block the return down low, at their feet.

As the match progresses, take note of the server's strengths and tendencies and adjust your position either up or back, and left or right. Many players serve to the same spot every single time, while others will give you a clue as to where they're serving by how they stand or where they toss the ball. For example, if the toss is to the left of the server's body, move to your left. If she tosses the ball wide to her right side, move to your right.

I even know one player who, without realizing it, actually looks to the area he's going to serve before he tosses the ball. The poor guy hasn't won his serve since the turn of the century and can't figure out why. If you can pick up a few of your opponent's tendencies you'll be able to get a quick jump on the serve and hit a stronger return

A quick turn

Just before contact, take your split step and see the ball come off your opponent's strings. Once you've determined which direction the serve is coming, immediately turn your shoulders and hips toward the oncoming ball.

A great drill to practice this quick turn, as well as early racket preparation, is to stand in your ready position as if you're about to receive serve. Imagine that the butt-cap of your racquet is glued to your belly button, pointing towards your opponent.

Take a split step and, as you're in the air, have a practice partner shout "forehand" or "backhand." As your feet touch down, immediately spring up and turn your shoulders and hips in the proper direction as quickly as you can. This will prepare your body and racket to react to the oncoming serve.

If your opponent has a big serve, use a short backswing and focus on pointing your strings to where you want the ball to go. Don't worry about generating speed. Let the server provide the juice—you simply control the ball.

If you're facing a serve that has little pace, the advantage now shifts to you, but you need to be careful to avoid the temptation to tee off and go for an outright winner. Very rarely will you be able to end the point with your return of serve, so don't try.

Instead, take control of the point by using a slightly bigger backswing and hit a deep, aggressive groundstroke. Or, you can block the ball back deep and move into the net. In both cases, take the ball early and be sure to use a long follow through. Focus on placement, not power. The momentum of your body moving into the shot will provide all the power you'll need.

Drills to practice your return

1.   Have your practice partner stand at his service line and serve to you. By moving closer, he'll be simulating a player with a big serve-and-volley game. Practice shortening your backswing and blocking the ball back. Aim for his shoes.

2.   Be sure to practice forehand and backhand returns from both the deuce and ad sides. Then switch with your partner and you do the serving while he practices his return.

3.   Practice receiving serves from two feet behind the service line. This will again simulate a big serve and help you improve your reaction time.

4.   Have your partner hit second serves from the baseline, and you practice hitting your return down the line and coming in. Play out the point. Play the first to 11. Be sure to practice both strokes, from both sides of the court, and then switch.

Adopt a "bring-it-on" attitude when receiving serve and show your opponent that you're not afraid of their power. Strive to get every serve back in play and take advantage of weak second serves. The serve is many players' biggest weapon and if you can take away that weapon with consistent, aggressive returns, you'll take away their heart and be well on your way to victory.

Chapter 7

Five Strokes
And You Win

Your groundstrokes are the foundation upon which the rest of your game is built, and whether you hit them with an Eastern grip and a closed stance, a Western grip and an open stance or an upside down grip standing on your head, your approach should always focus on consistency.

This requires a mental shift because much of what we hear, see and read about tennis tells us to "go for it" with our groundstrokes. While this approach may light up our tennis lives for a brief moment, over the course of a long two- or three-set match, this strategy usually brings far more pain than pleasure.

I want you to remember that groundstrokes are not meant to be point ending shots but rather point building shots. Winners hit from the baseline are extremely rare, and trying to end the point from the backcourt will wear you out physically and emotionally.

When you watch a boxing match between two great champions, you see each fighter circle the ring, probing for openings. This is the approach to bring to your groundstrokes. Let your opponent go for the Mike Tyson, big-shot style, while you emulate boxing legend Muhammad Ali and build your attack with consistency and shot combinations. This approach will slowly but surely wear your opponent down and allow you to ultimately move in for the knockout.

Refuse to miss

Consistency is a mindset. So the next time you step on the court, do so with a "refuse-to- miss" attitude. Forget about the big shots and keep the ball in play. If you can hit the ball in the court five times each point, you'll probably beat 90 percent of the players who are beating you now

Here are three easy-to-implement strategies that will immediately make you a steadier player from the baseline:

1.   Clear the net. Clearing the net is your first concern, so I want you to develop three different heights from which you can hit your groundstrokes. The first is a "rally height," about 5-6 feet over the net, used when you are in a baseline exchange where no one has the advantage. Next is a "defensive height,"15-20 feet over the net, used when you are in trouble. Finally develop an "offensive height," 1-2 feet over the net, and use it when you are attacking a short ball or hitting a passing shot.

2.   Stay away from the lines. Never, ever aim for the lines. Australian coaching legend Harry Hopman was famous for telling his players to "hit for the lines." With all due respect to Hop, I say that unless your name is Laver, Sharapova or Federer, forget about the lines. Always give yourself at least a 3-5-foot margin of safety.

3.   Hit the majority of your groundstrokes cross-court. You'll be hitting over the lowest part of the net, the middle. The court is also longer on the diagonal, giving you a larger margin for error.

15-20 feet

5-6 feet

1-2 feet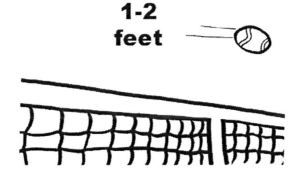

Controlled Groundstrokes

Spin your way to the next level

If consistency is the hallmark of a good tennis player, the ability to add spin to your groundstrokes is what will take that consistency to the next level.   Spin has the reputation of being some kind of mysterious, complex trick that only advanced players can use. Actually, the physics of spin are quite simple, and believe it or not, you're already using it.

Many players think they hit a "flat" ball, but the fact is it's virtually impossible to hit a ball that has no rotation. Coaching legend Vic Braden says that a ball that is moving through the air "generates air pockets, and air friction from those pockets makes the ball do certain things. Good tennis players deliberately control this ball rotation and use it to their advantage." In other words, if you can learn to use the various spins, your levels of both control and consistency will rise dramatically.

Flavors of spin

Topspin is king today and virtually every player in the world uses it to some degree. To put topspin on the ball you need to swing your racket in a low-to-high motion. If the ball were the face of a clock, topspin rotation would bring 6:00 over 12:00 as the ball moved away from you.

A ball hit with topspin will initially rise and then, very quickly, fall. The nature of the spin pulls the ball down, so topspin allows you to swing harder, aim higher, and still keep the ball in the court. When the ball does bounce, your opponent will feel as if it's jumping right on top of them. This is why many people refer to topspin as the "power" spin.

Topspin should be your spin of choice for the vast majority of your groundstrokes because it allows you to hit a strong ball four feet or more above the net and still keep it deep in your opponent's backcourt.

If you are primarily a doubles player, you do need to be careful how high you hit over the net due to the opposing team's net player. Anything more than a foot or two above the net is likely to get picked off and volleyed away by an alert opponent. When playing doubles, keep the majority of your groundstrokes at either the offensive (1-2 feet over the net) or defensive (15-20 feet) heights.

Slice is nice

In our power-obsessed world, topspin gets the glory. However, slice, though not as fast moving, can be just as devastating a weapon as a ball hit with topspin. Steffi Graf is proof of this. Her slice backhand helped her become one of the most dominant women players in history.

As a ball hit with topspin falls, a ball hit with slice will rise, which means that the harder it's hit, the more likely it is to float up in the air. This is not a good thing, as floating balls are easy prey for an aggressive opponent.

In addition, a ball hit with slice will travel through the air slower than one hit with topspin, which is why slice is more of a control and finesse spin. When a ball hit well with slice bounces, it stays low, making it great for approach shots and drop shots, as the spin will pull the ball back toward the net after it lands.

Though topspin gets all of the press today, don't ignore the potential of slice to enhance both your control and consistency. A few years ago, I was teaching at a corporate event in California. A friend of mine named Larry, who was coaching several touring pros at the time, was also at the event and was working with a middle-aged salesman named Barry.

Barry, a 3.0 level player who played once or twice a week, was terribly frustrated because he couldn't hit his backhand with any consistency. He'd taken hours of lessons at his local club to no avail, and it was widely known that if you wanted to beat Barry, all you had to do was hit the ball to his backhand and he would self-destruct.

For three days I watched my friend try to teach this man a topspin backhand. They hit thousands of balls, with about one out of 50 successfully going over the net and in the court. As you might expect, their frustration levels were rising. Finally, on the fourth day as we were walking to the courts, Larry said to me, "I can't face another day with this guy. You give it a try."

"Okay, I'll take a shot," I told him.

When Barry walked onto the court and saw me, he immediately smiled and said, "What's the matter? Larry couldn't take it anymore?" We both laughed.

Then we began to hit back and forth, and right off the bat, Barry told me about his "backhand issue." He was right, his backhand was terrible.

Each time I would hit to Barry's forehand, he looked relaxed, confident and stroked the ball back with consistent depth. As soon as I hit one to his backhand, I could see the panic in his eyes as he tried to remember everything his pros had told him and anything that might bail him out. He hit the frame, the fence, the lake behind the fence. You name it and Barry put a ball there— anywhere but in the court.

I looked over to the next court at Larry, who was smiling and winking at me as he was hitting with a couple of pretty women. He was mouthing the words, "Are you having fun yet?"

After breaking the ice with a few jokes, I asked Barry about all the instruction he'd had. He said that he'd tried everything to improve his backhand. He'd tried both a one-hander and a two-hander. He'd gotten into tremendous shape so that he could run around his backhand and avoid hitting it altogether. He even tried a left-handed forehand. That was how desperate he was.

It seemed like he'd tried everything—everything that is, but a slice backhand. When I suggested the slice to Barry, he immediately made a face as if he smelled a skunk. "Slice is for wimps," he said.

After showing Barry a few of my slice backhands which, though not as good as Steffi's, have always been among my better shots, and convincing him that "real men" do hit with slice, he agreed to give it a try. After all, what did he have to lose?

I showed him the basics, and after about 50 balls he started to get a bit of a feel for it. Within 25 minutes, he was actually able to rally back and forth with his new backhand. Was it pretty? No. Did it go in the court? A vast majority of the time, it did. Needless to say, he was thrilled and couldn't wait to try out his new backhand on his buddies back home.

There's a cute ending to the story. Three months after our lesson, I received an envelope in the mail. In it was a picture of Barry holding up his 3.0 league championship trophy. At the bottom of the photo he had written, "Match point—slice backhand down the line for a winner. Real men do hit with slice. Thanks!"

Give it time to develop

When you venture into the world of slice and topspin, keep in mind that there are varying degrees of spin. Trial and error will help you develop the proper feel so that you can put as much or as little spin on the ball as the situation dictates.

You may be in for quite a few laughs when your first attempts at hitting topspin hit you in the foot, or your first attempts at slice come back and hit you in the chest.

Remember, it's all part of the process of learning, and with practice you'll master the techniques of hitting with spin. As you practice you'll begin to see that there are more and more things you can do with the ball, depending upon how much, or how little, spin you apply.

Whether it's Roger Federer, Maria Sharapova or Betty from down the block, the best players in the world, and at your club, all have one thing in common: a strong base of consistency and an understanding of how slice and topspin contribute to that consistency.

The next time you take the court with that annoying rival who's beaten you the last four times, remind yourself to aim higher over the net and stay away from the lines. Use topspin and slice to help you control the ball and let your opponent go for the "big" shot. I think you'll be pleasantly surprised at the results.

OPEN OR CLOSED?

Once upon a time, every player hit groundstrokes with a closed stance in which the shoulders and hips are turned away from the net to face the sideline. The advent of lighter weight rackets and the popularity of Western-style grips have allowed players to remain in an open stance, hips facing the net to hit their groundstrokes, as long as they rotate their upper bodies during the stroke.

By "opening up" we're told that it's easier to get into position and we can generate more racket head speed, which, of course, means more topspin and power. Most of the touring professionals today use an open stance and, consequently, it's taught by many teaching pros.

Aside from the "coolness" factor of trying to hit the ball like the pros, I think many recreational players use the open stance as a crutch because it requires less footwork— less footwork, but far more athleticism and skill. Take a look around and you see players of all ages with their Western grips, wide-open stances and exaggerated topspin strokes hitting ball after ball off their frames and then sprinting for the ice machine and Advil because their arms are throbbing.

If you haven't yet guessed, I prefer the closed stance for both the forehand and backhand. I think it offers more options and it's easier on our arms. Also, recent studies by Vic Braden have shown that the open stance does not provide more racket head speed through the hitting zone as has been suggested.

Sure, the closed stance requires more footwork, but that's the name of the game. If you're really struggling to reach a ball, the open stance can bail you out—just don't use it as an excuse for laziness.

Chapter 8

Jackpot At The Net

Rick is a 43-year-old writer who had been playing tennis for four years. Aching to move up to the next level he knew that he could no longer win strictly from the backcourt. He wanted to learn how to play the net. So, after a few lessons going over the various aspects of net play, Rick felt he was ready to "charge large," as he put it.

The following week, Rick came to his lesson wearing a chest protector and helmet. The first words out of his mouth were, "I thought you said that the player who gets to the net controls the point." Rick was shell-shocked. He'd made his way to the net and found that things happen much faster up close where the good players live.

We can all sympathize with Rick's plight. The net can be a frightening place. You're much closer to your opponent and the ball's coming at you twice as fast. Scary as it may seem, with a little knowledge and practice the net can feel as comfortable to you as your favorite pair of tennis shoes.

Successful net play begins with understanding when to move in and then, what to do once you're up there.

As soon as possible

This is my response when my students ask me when they should go to the net. Each time you or your opponent strikes the ball, ask yourself the following question: "Can I move in on this shot?"

Don't be afraid of the net.

A good way to decide is to divide the tennis court into sections using the example of a traffic light. The area behind, the baseline is the red light; the area between the baseline and service line is the yellow light; and the area from the service line to the net is the green light.

If you are standing in the red zone to hit the ball, Stop! Stay back, hit a groundstroke and wait for a better opportunity. If you are standing in the yellow zone, Proceed with Caution! The ball may be short enough to attack, but you may not be able to hit a strong enough approach shot or get close enough to the net to volley effectively. If you are standing in the green zone to hit the ball, Go! You've got a green light, so hit your approach and get to the net.

Experienced players have learned to anticipate a short ball from their opponent a shot or two before it actually occurs. They understand that what causes a player to hit short is basically one of two things: either a strong shot by them or a weak stroke by their opponent.

If you know that Bill hasn't hit a strong backhand in the last 10 years, and you put a deep shot into his backhand corner, get ready to rumble. Or, if you get a soft floater that bounces up about waist high into your strike zone, hit a firm shot and look for the short reply. In fact, any time you hit a shot that makes your opponent scramble, take a quick step or two inside the baseline in anticipation.

Yes, I know you're now standing on the edge of the dreaded "no-man's land," but that's okay. The danger of standing in "no-mans land" is that your opponent will drive a hard shot down at your feet or past you. However, when she's stretched out, off-balance or on the run the chances of this are slim. Her return will most likely be weak, and you can then attack with an approach shot or volley.

Incidentally, if your opponent ever turns her back to you to run after a ball, immediately move a few steps forward. The best she will be able to do under those circumstances is to put up a lob, and you'll be in position to put away the volley or overhead

What are they going to do?

When you stake your claim to the net, your first priority is to figure out whether your opponent is going to lob or drive their shot. To do so, pay attention to their body and racket. If they're leaning forward as they approach the ball and their racket face is flat or slightly closed, pointing down to the court, they're probably going to drive the ball. Immediately take two quick steps forward and prepare to volley. If you notice your opponent leaning back with his racket face open, strings pointing toward the sky, a lob is not far behind. Quickly take three steps back.

The keys to winning volleys

If you watch great net players like Martina Navratilova or Roger Federer, you'll see that they all have two things in common: they keep their hands up around chest height and their feet "angry."

As soon as you've determined that you'll have to hit a volley, quickly move forward. The closer you can get to the net, the easier the ball is to put away. Push your racket out, with your strings pointing toward your target, and simply let the ball hit the strings.

My old college coach, Norm Copeland, developed a great drill to help us keep our backswing short on the volley. Norm would line us up at the baseline, holding our rackets out in front of us in the forehand volley position. He'd then yell, "Go," and we would sprint to the net, split step as Norm fed us a forehand volley. We would then move forward and hit a deep volley toward a target, but we were not allowed to move our arms an inch. While this drill was a bit extreme—you generally jab your racket 5-10 inches on the volley—the point was clearly driven home: you do not volley with your arm. You volley with your feet and your hands!

A fun drill to develop this moving forward mentality, as well as a short volley motion, is to hit up-close volleys with a friend. Stand on opposite sides of the net, each of you about a foot inside the service line. Put the ball in play and volley back and forth without letting the ball touch the ground. After each shot, move in a step so that you get closer and closer to each other. As you both get on top of the net, try to catch the ball in between your two rackets.

Skilled net players are always trying to move forward. During my clinics, I tell my students that if the ball bounces in front of them when they're at the net, they owe me a dollar. I also tell them that with two kids to put through college, I'll be collecting those dollars at the end of the class.

Keep in mind that most volley errors occur on the first volley when players will often try to put the ball away. Rarely will your first volley be a put-away shot. As you approach the net, plan on hitting at least two volleys.

Volleying is not for swingers

The volley is perhaps the shot that has suffered the most in this age of "wham-bam, o- damn-I-missed" tennis. What's the hot "new" shot on the pro tour? The swinging volley.

Usually played somewhere around or behind the service line, the swinging volley is in essence a groundstroke that you hit before it bounces. It can be a tremendously powerful, point-ending shot but it requires superb timing and has a huge potential for error.

In my opinion, the swinging volley is an impatient shot. When you have the opportunity, hit the ball in the air from the mid-court or further back, don't try to end the point with one shot. Hit an approach volley, move into the net and win the point with a higher percentage volley or overhead.

Leave the swinging, power volleys to Serena and Maria. Keep your hands up, feet angry and motion short.

The slam dunk overhead

An opponent's lob evokes one of two thoughts in a tennis player's mind: Either "Yeah, baby!" or "Oh no!" Good players love it when their opponent lobs because it usually means that they'll get to hit an overhead smash. Lower level players hate to see lobs because they know how difficult overheads can be to execute and are afraid that they're not going to be able to get the ball back in play.

Once you see the lob go up, immediately swing your right leg back and turn your shoulders and hips in the same direction. At the same time, bring your racket straight up past your right ear, like when you pick up a telephone, and place it into the "backscratch" position.

As your right arm moves behind your head, place your left index finger up and point at the oncoming ball. This will help you follow the ball and position yourself. If you notice that your left arm is moving back over your head, this means that the lob is deep and you have to back up more. If your index finger is falling in front of you, it means that you have to move back in toward the net.

Do your best to hit the ball while it's still in the air. Hitting your overhead before it bounces gives your opponent less time to recover and anticipate your shot. In addition, if you let the ball bounce, it will usually bounce farther away from the net, making your overhead more difficult to execute.

An exception to this would be if you're playing outside and your opponent hits a high, defensive lob into the stratosphere. The higher the lob, the faster it falls and the more difficult it is for you to time. The "moonball" lob will still bounce high enough for you to hit an aggressive overhead. Also, if you're looking into the sun, you may want to let the ball bounce to give you a bit more time to prepare. Be sure to use your left hand to shield your eyes from the sun.

If you don't feel that you can get back in time to hit a balanced overhead, simply turn the shot into a volley. Take the ball out of the air, and punch it back deep. Then move back into the net.

There will be times when your opponent's lob is just too good for you to take out of the air. In this case, run back as quickly as you can and try to get behind the ball. Don't run directly at the ball, but rather circle around it.

As you're moving back, briefly take your eyes off the ball and take a quick look at your opponent. If he stays in the backcourt after lobbing, there's no pressure on your shot. Simply lob the ball back and move into position for a baseline rally.

If you see him charging the net after lobbing—as a good player should—you now have to come up with a good shot. More often than not, this will be another lob. Make him hit the physically challenging overhead.

If you get back in time to set up behind the ball, you can consider driving a passing shot but if you feel off balance in any way, throw up a lob, keep it deep and make him hit an overhead. Remember, always give your opponent the opportunity to hand you the point with an error.

Many players spend their tennis lives glued to the baseline playing defensive tennis. While this strategy will allow you to win a lot of matches against lower level players, if you want to rub shoulders with the big boys and girls at your club, leave your fear in your racket bag and make the journey to the net. As your anticipation and volley and overhead skills improve you're going to find a lot more matches ending in your favor.

Chapter 9

Two Shots
That Deserve Respect

They're the Rodney Dangerfield shots of tennis and players who use them get no respect. They're ridiculed, looked down upon, and yet can be two of your most devastating weapons. I'm talking about the lob and drop shot.

Love the lob

If you watch a match between players at the 2.0 to 3.0 levels, you'll see a lob-fest: one lob right after another. Players at this level are just learning to rally, so they lob back and forth and have a great time keeping the ball in play.

Now check out a match between players at the 3.5 to 4.0 levels, and you'll frequently see an entirely different

> *People make fun of those players who like to throw up a lob every two or three shots, but they seem to forget that good lobbers have more trophies than any other person at the club.*
>
> Vic Braden
> Master teaching pro

brand of tennis. These players have learned to hit the ball harder and have found that they can occasionally come up with that impressive, big-time shot that everyone craves. As I've said, that feeling is addictive and many players come to feel that because they can hit the ball hard, they must hit the ball hard—on every shot.

So, they push aside the lob with a condescending sneer, opting instead to go for that once-in-a-blue-moon winner they see the pros hit on TV. The problem, however, is that this attempt at the great shot more often than not results in an error. Tennis at this level can be characterized as a race to see who can miss enough shots to lose the match first.

Now fast forward to a 4.5 to 5.0 level match. What do you see? Long, exciting points with—you got it—lots of lobs! These players have gotten over the ego boost of hitting that rare world-class shot and have learned that the lob is one of the most effective weapons in the game.

Reduce your errors immediately

One of the biggest differences between 3.5-level players and those at the higher levels is that the stronger players simply make fewer errors. While the lob has many uses from both offensive and defensive standpoints, what makes it a tennis player's best friend is that it enables us to cut down on our errors.

Many errors are a result of trying the wrong shot at the wrong time. While 3.5 players are still trying to conquer the tennis world with their net skimming, line cleaning shots, the 5.0s realize that winning tennis does not consist of a few great shots but rather a lot of pretty good ones.

These players have shifted their focus away from the "big shot" mentality and moved toward point development. They patiently keep the ball in play, move it around, probe for weaknesses and, above all, refuse to miss. Instead of trying the high-risk, impressive-looking power shot when they're off balance, they'll simply throw up a high, deep lob. This strategy significantly reduces their errors.

Hit Up

Anytime you feel uncomfortable with your position to the ball or situation on the court, recite the words "hit up" to yourself. Get the ball back over the net and force your opponent to hit another shot to win the point. Even the shortest, weakest lob is better than an error, because by forcing your opponent to hit that extra shot you're giving them one more opportunity to miss. You'll be amazed at how often they'll accommodate you.

Chasing down lobs and hitting overheads are two of the most physically demanding and frustrating skills in the game to master. Even if your lob is put away, you've still made your opponent hit an extra shot. And if you can force them to hit two or three overheads to end a point, their tongue will eventually be dragging.

An additional advantage of the lob is that it will keep a net-rusher guessing. Many "macho" players are stubborn and refuse to lob. Their opponents know this so they charge the net like a bull in a china shop. By throwing up the occasional lob, you're telling your net rushing opponent that he must always be aware of the possibility of a lob. With this thought in his head, he won't charge as aggressively or get as close to the net.

Different kinds of lobs

There are two types of lobs—offensive and defensive. An offensive lob should set you up to win the point, while a defensive lob is designed to keep you in the point. For example, your opponent hits a strong approach shot and you have to scramble just to reach it. Rather than try a low-percentage passing shot from an awkward position on the court with the ball out of your strike zone, throw up a high, defensive lob and make him hit the ball to beat you.

Hit up

A defensive lob might not even go over your opponent's head but by hitting it very high, preferably deep and crosscourt where the court is 6.2 feet longer crosscourt, you're giving yourself time to recover your position or catch your breath while your opponent has to decide how to play the ball. If he goes for the overhead, he'll have a tough time, because the higher the ball has been hit, the faster it will fall, making the shot tougher to time.

More often than not, if you hit a lob high and deep enough, your opponent will be forced to let it bounce. Then he will have to back away from the net even more to either hit the overhead or play the ball back with a groundstroke. Either way, you'll have pushed him off the net and into a less threatening position, while at the same time giving yourself time to recover.

An offensive surprise

The time to hit an offensive lob is when you're in control of your shot and a lob is the last thing your opponent's expecting. Let's say she's come to the net behind a short approach shot. As you move forward, she's likely to anticipate a passing shot and move closer to the net. This is the ideal time to surprise her with a lob.

The offensive lob should not be hit as high as the defensive lob and should go just over the net player's outstretched racket. This will give the ball a low bounce, making it extremely difficult for your opponent to chase down. Think of the offensive lob as your third passing shot option. When your opponent attacks the net, you can pass her down the line, crosscourt or over her head.

I frequently use the lob as my first option when I'm under attack, particularly during the first few games of a match. I want to test my opponent's movement and overhead skills and, if I can make them hit a few overheads early in the match, I've begun the process of tiring them out. Lots of players hit strong overheads the first four or five games of the match but, after that, are so tired they can barely lift their rackets above their heads.

Finally, remember that your opponent doesn't need to be charging the net for you to hit a lob. A high lob in the middle of a rally can serve several purposes. It changes the pace of the ball, the rhythm of the rally, and, perhaps most important of all, it can give you a bit of a breather while the point is still in play. Jimmy Connors was a master at this, particularly at the end of his career.

There are a lot of shots in tennis that would be nice to have, for example, a 140-mph serve or an atomic forehand, but that you don't really need to be a winning player. You do need to have a good lob because not only can it get you out of a tight situation, it can also be your most devastating weapon.

A dagger in their hearts

I absolutely love the drop shot, because it works so well in combination with the lob—and it drives opponents crazy. A lob followed by a drop shot, or vice versa, is a great way to chop down those macho-man big hitters that we all come up against.

You can hit a drop shot with a forehand, a backhand or a volley. The motion is similar to scooping ice cream out of a box. It's an exaggerated slice where you bring your racket from a high to low position. At contact you want to "scoop" under the ball. This adds backspin, which slows the ball down and can even make it bounce backward if enough spin is applied.

Ideally, the best place to attempt a drop shot is when you're at or near the service line and your opponent is back on his baseline. The farther from the net you are, the more difficult the shot is to execute, and the more time your opponent has to react to it.

A key element of the drop shot is surprise, so you want to make your opponent think that you're going to "drive" the ball rather than "drop" it. Use your normal backswing but instead of driving through the ball, at the last instant "scoop" under it for the drop. The drop shot is a "touch" shot that requires a lot of practice to get the proper "feel." One of the best ways to develop this "feel" is to play mini-tennis.

When you're playing singles, aim the majority of your drop shots down the line. Even though you're hitting over the highest part of the net, the ball will travel a shorter distance giving your opponent less time to react, plus you're keeping the ball in front of you, which will better position you to respond to the next shot.

Here's a play that will drive your opponents crazy. Hit a drop shot as an approach shot. Imagine this scenario: The last three times Nancy hit a short ball to you, you moved in, hit a deep approach shot to her backhand corner and rushed the net.

Now, she's hit another short ball and as you move in to attack, what do you think Nancy's going to expect? Of course, another deep ball to the corner. So, as she backs up in anticipation, you toss in a drop shot and follow it up to the net.

Even if Nancy can respond quickly enough to reach your drop shot, she now has to contend with you at the net. It's a great tactic to keep your opponent off balance. Just be sure that you are well inside the baseline line when you try it.

You won't use the drop shot as much playing doubles because you generally don't want to draw your opponents in to the net. However, when both members of the opposing team are at the baseline, the shot can be an effective weapon.

A lot of big hitters scoff at the lob and drop shot and will give you a dirty look when you use "touch shots" to beat them. Ignore them! What they're basically saying is that you shouldn't hit those shots because they don't want to run for them. Remember, movement is just as important a skill as strokes—more so in my mind.

If your opponent hasn't developed the movement skills to cover the lob or drop shot—that's a polite way of saying he is out of shape or slow—take advantage of it and don't be embarrassed.

When you face a player with a weak backhand, where do you hit the ball? To his backhand, of course! So if your competition doesn't move well, use that to your advantage. Lob 'em and drop shot 'em till they drop!

WHY MINI-TENNIS IS GOOD FOR YOU?

You stand at the service line on your side of the court and your practice partner does the same. You rally back and forth, keeping the ball inside the four service boxes.

Aside from being a great warm-up exercise, mini-tennis offers something for players of all ages and abilities. It enables 1.0 to 2.5-level players to immediately get the idea of hitting the ball over the net and gain confidence in their ability to rally.

Tennis professional Peter Burwash has written that he "taught a 3-year-old boy and a man of 80 to hit 100 balls in a row over the net in their first hour of tennis" through mini-tennis. For 3.0 to 4.0 players, mini-tennis allows them to work on their touch, consistency and understanding of point development. By having to keep the ball within the service lines, power is taken out of the equation. You must win your points by maneuvering the other player around the court.

For the 4.5 players and above, mini-tennis allows them to do the same. Without power it's very difficult to end a point, so the rallies in mini-tennis tend to be very long with lots of quick starts and stops.

When I was in college, we used play mini-tennis matches. Not only did we enhance our control, we also got a great workout and had a lot of fun! Here's a mini-tennis program to get you started.

1. Rally down the line as many times as you can.
2. Rally crosscourt as many times as you can.
3. Rally full court mini-tennis, using both service boxes. Try to move each other around.
4. Play first to 21 points. Singles or doubles

Some players brush mini-tennis aside, calling it "baby tennis." Roger Federer, Martina Navratilova and a few others I've seen play it would disagree.

Chapter 10

Trumping Tennis's Toughest Shots

There are four shots in the game that strike fear into the hearts of the mortal tennis player. Though they're awkward to execute, with a few tips and a "just-get-it-back" approach, you'll be able to handle them and often surprise your opponents by returning a shot they thought they'd hit for a winner.

The half-volley

A half-volley, or pick-up, is that annoying shot you have to play when a ball bounces right at your feet. You can't move forward quickly enough to hit it out of the air, and it bounces too close to you to hit a proper groundstroke. It's literally half a volley and half a groundstroke.

Usually we get caught having to play a half-volley when we approach the net and our opponent drops the ball at our feet. Sometimes, however, we have to hit a half-volley when we're standing inside our own baseline and our opponent hits a deep groundstroke right at us.

Your goal when hitting the half-volley is to just get it back in play. With an extremely short backswing or no backswing at all, keep a firm wrist, bend at the knees and lower yourself to the level of the ball, keeping your racket out in front of you.

As soon as the ball hits the ground, keep your racket face square or just slightly open. The feeling is that of gently lifting the ball over the net. Your stroke should be more of a push than a swing. Stay low and use a slight, and I repeat slight, upward motion.

A good exercise to practice the half-volley is to say the words "boom boom" to yourself as fast as you can when hitting the shot. This will give you a feel for the rhythm involved and will also improve your timing.

Don't try to hit a winner off the half-volley, just get it back and then move into the net for you next shot or back behind the baseline so you won't have to hit another one

The backhand overhead

French Open Champion Rafael Nadel makes it look easy, but for most of us the backhand overhead can be the toughest shot in the game. It's another of those just-get-it-back shots, so don't try to do anything fancy or aggressive with it. Just put the ball back in play and go from there.

When your opponent lofts a short lob over your backhand shoulder, if you react quickly enough, many times you can run around it and hit your regular overhead. However, if you must play the ball on your backhand side, I suggest turning the shot into a volley.

Immediately turn your body and wait for the ball to drop into your volley strike zone. Using a short backswing, simply punch the ball back deep and begin to look for your opponent's next shot.

Right at you

How often have you been at the net and your opponent blasts the ball right at you? This happens quite frequently, particularly in doubles, and is, in fact, an excellent strategy that often handcuffs the net player.

So, how do you avoid that deer-in-the-headlights syndrome when you're an easy target for your opponents body shot? Ideally, when a ball is coming right at your

Right at You

body, try to move to one side and play either a comfortable forehand or backhand volley.

Often, however, you won't have the time to move. In that case, keep your wrist firm and play a backhand. That's really the only way you can physically get the racket in front of your body without severely and dangerously contorting your arm. Squeeze your grip tightly and just let the ball hit the strings.

The backfire or over the shoulder shot

A topspin lob goes over your head and you know right away that you're in trouble. You can't take the ball in the air, and getting behind it to hit a controlled stroke is just not in the cards. You're going to have to hit the shot in front of your body with your back to the net. Now what?

Illie Nastase, one of the most talented players ever to grip a racket, made famous a shot he called the "Bucharest Backfire" for just this situation. Line yourself up so that when the ball bounces, it's over your left shoulder (if you are right handed; for lefties, it's the opposite shoulder). Then swing your arm and flick your wrist up into the ball over your left shoulder. A Continental grip is the best for this shot as it gives you a bit more flexibility in your wrist.

You can hit any kind of shot with a backfire, from a high defensive lob to a low offensive drive that just clears the net. It all depends on how athletic and aggressive you want to be on the court. For most of us, however, our goal here is just to get the ball back with a high lob and stay in the point.

Though these four shots may never be your biggest weapons they don't need to be major weaknesses. By using simple techniques and the just-get-it-back approach, you can return these difficult balls and stay alive while you wait for your opportunity to take control of the point.

Chapter 11

When To Turn On
The Power

Now, the moment you've been waiting for: a chapter on power. Once you've developed the ability to consistently place your shots where you want, adding power to those shots can be the icing on the cake.

You don't need to swing hard to hit hard

Have you ever noticed that skinny 10-year-old at the club who hits the ball a ton? As the kid rips one groundstroke after another, yet still manages to keep the ball in the court, you say to yourself, "I'm much stronger than that little runt, so how come every time I try to hit with power my shots end up in the next area code?"

The fact is, controlled power does not come from big muscles or by swinging hard at the ball. In fact, a harder swing frequently produces a slower moving ball! This is true because when we take a big, hard swing the muscles in our arm tense up. This tenseness often causes us to lose control of our racket face resulting in mis-hit, slower moving balls.

Most advanced players and professionals usually swing their arms at roughly 75 percent of their capability. At this percentage they're able to keep their racket face stable and therefore their shots, under control.

In order to add power to your shots you need to increase the speed of your racket head as it makes contact with the ball. This is best done by coordinating your legs,

"How does she hit so hard?"

hips, trunk and shoulders, so that they work together to propel your racket into the ball. This coordination is called your kinetic chain and it means simply using the different links in the chain—legs, hips, trunk, and shoulders, arms and wrist, to transfer energy from one part to the other.

Let's say you wanted to add a little juice to your forehand. Wait for a ball that's in your strike zone between your waist and knees. As you prepare, coil your shoulders, trunk and hips and bend your knees. As you begin your swing, simply uncoil the parts.

The energy is then transferred through your body, building at each link in the chain. It moves up from your legs, through your hips, trunk, shoulder, arms and wrist, finally reaching your racket.

The end result is a faster moving racket head that transfers speed onto your shot. This is how that skinny little kid, and the pros, generate so much power and still maintain their control.

For those of you who simply can't wait to venture into the world of the big hitter, there are a few equipment adjustments you can make that will automatically give your shots more pace. Here are three:

1. Buy a stiffer racket. A stiffer racket will provide more power. There are many on the market today that are both stiffer and lighter. Ask your pro or local tennis shop for advice.

2. String your racket looser. This will also give your shots a boost. Begin by stringing your racket three to five pounds looser and see how it feels.

3. Add lead tape. Lead tape placed around various areas of your racket's head will make the racket heavier and therefore put more force behind your strokes.

These are simply shortcuts to power and may cause you to suffer a loss of control for a while. When all is said and done, the best and most reliable source of power is improved technique and use of your kinetic chain.

When to add power

The serve is the defining shot of the power player and throughout history we've seen some big ones. To date, Andy Roddick holds the record for the fastest serve ever hit at 155 mph, while for the ladies, Venus Williams fired in a record serve of 127.4 mph. While you may not reach the 100-mph mark on the radar gun, a more powerful serve can win you some easy points as well as intimidate an opponent.

There's an old saying in tennis that "you're only as good as your second serve" and, like most old sayings, there's an element of truth to it. If your second serve is weak, you need to be particularly focused on getting a high percentage of first serves in. Save the power serves for the less important points, such as 40-0 or 0-40. These are points that you can afford to lose so you can take a bit of a risk and go for the rocket serve.

If you're up 40-0 and happen to get your big one in, it's a nice exclamation point to the game. If you're down 0-40 and throw in a bomb, you may just intimidate your opponent enough to get you back in the game. If you've developed a strong second serve, you can be a bit more aggressive on your first, so go for the big one now and then.

Here are a few of the most common shot situations in which you might want to "crank it up" on your groundstrokes:

- When you have a ball in the mid-court that's in your strike zone.
- Hitting a passing shot when your opponent's at the net.
- Returning a weak second serve from your opponent

Do not to add power to your shot:

1. If you're more than four feet behind the baseline
2. If you're more than four feet outside of the court
3. If the ball is out of your strike zone.
4. If the ball is inside the service line and below the height of the net.

In all of these situations, you are out of position either relative to the court or the ball, so simply play the ball back safely and wait for another opportunity.

Power can be a devastating weapon if it's achieved properly and unleashed at the right time. Continue to work on your strokes in practice and you'll find that, as your timing and technique improve, your shots will become more powerful and difficult for your opponents to handle.

Part 3

Good Thinking Tops Great Strokes

You may not take many lessons or have the most beautiful strokes at the courts, but that doesn't mean you can't be a winning tennis player. Brad Gilbert proved this during his 12-year career on the pro tour.

Though a frustrated opponent once compared his strokes to "a caveman who found a tennis racket," Gilbert notched wins over such players as John McEnroe, Boris Becker, Pete Sampras, Jimmy Connors and Andre Agassi, to name a few. Ranked in the top ten for five years, he reached a career high of number 4 in the world in 1990.

Gilbert, whose style of play was frequently described as "winning ugly," says in his book of the same title that "pretty strokes are okay. But there's a lot more to the game than that."

Tennis matches aren't won by the players with the nicest looking strokes but rather by those who don't beat themselves, who understand the percentages, analyze their opponent's games and come up with a game plan for victory.

In this section of the book you'll learn to become a better player by becoming a more intelligent player. You'll see that, up until the 4.0 level it really makes no difference who's standing on the opposite side of

> *I call tennis the "lazy man's game" now. Guys rely on giant serves and huge groundstrokes, but little thought, strategy or passion goes into it.*
>
> John McEnroe
> Six-time Grand Slam singles champion

the net. I'm going to show you a progressive approach to tennis strategy that will begin by showing you how to defeat the tennis devil that exists inside us all. You'll see that as your game improves and you face tougher opponents, you'll need to change your strategies accordingly.

Chapter 12

Conquering
Our Inner Devil

How many times have you said to yourself after a particularly horrendous error, "Why did I try that crazy shot when all I needed to do was get the ball back in the court?" Chances are, the reason you tried that "crazy" shot was that your Tennis Devil got the better of you.

For many players, particularly those of us between the 2.0-3.5 levels, our toughest competition doesn't come from the player standing on the opposite side of the net but rather from the opposition between our ears. I call it our Tennis Devil and when the match gets tight or things don't go our way, he springs to life and uses his weapons— impatience, anger and fear—to take over our minds and destroy our games.

When our Devil takes over, we begin to try low percentage shots, committing one unforced error after another. We angrily slam balls into the fence and, when the big point arrives, are so nervous we can't lift our arms to serve. Before we know it, the match is over and we've beaten ourselves! Impatience, fear and anger are opponents we all face, but with a few simple strategies we can learn to push them aside and still play a winning game.

Polish up your patience

Chris Evert once said, "ninety percent of my game is mental. It's my concentration that has gotten me this far." Many players struggle with their concentration and, after

"Hit it harder, Dummy!"

two or three shots, lose their patience and take unnecessary risks. Consistency drills are a great way to improve your patience, call it mental endurance, and cut down on your unforced errors.

When I was learning the game, I would walk onto the court, warm up, and my coach would say, "Okay, let's start off with 20 crosscourt forehands beyond the service line." I would stand in one corner, my coach in the opposite, and we'd begin to rally, back and forth, until we hit 20 in a row beyond the service line.

If I accomplished the goal, we moved on to another consistency drill. If not, we kept trying until I did, even if it took the entire hour. Through drills such as these, which I still do thirty years later, I developed mental endurance by learning to keep the ball in play for an extended period of time.

Do you remember the fabulous Gene Hackman movie Hoosiers? Hackman portrayed a down-on-his-luck basketball coach in a small town in Indiana. To teach his out of control team the value of patience, he insisted that, each time down the floor, they pass the ball at least three times before they even thought about taking a shot.

To take that concept to the next level, during your next match, tell yourself that you're going to hit five balls back before trying to win the point. As you hit each shot, actually count to yourself, "one, two, three, four, five." This will help you increase your level of patience and you'll also be amazed at how often hitting just a few shots in the court will win the point.

High-level players have the mental endurance of a marathoner and are prepared to hit as many shots as it takes to win the point. Patience made Hackman's Hoosiers winners and it will do the same for you.

It's tough to hit the ball with your hands around your throat

Tennis players come in all shapes, sizes and abilities, but we all have one thing in common—when the pressure is on, our nerves and muscles tighten up and don't work like they should. Be it a social doubles game, a league match or a tournament final, whenever the score is being kept, the opportunity to get angry at ourselves or "choke" always hovers in the air.

There wasn't a tennis fan in the world that didn't ache for Jana Novotna after her heartbreaking loss to Steffi Graf in the 1993 Wimbledon ladies singles final. Serving in the third set up 4-1, 40-30, Novotna was just five points away from the game's most coveted title when her Tennis Devil got the better of her. A few agonizing minutes later, she collapsed in tears as the Duchess of Kent handed her the runner-up prize. Novotna had choked—big time!

We choke because we're afraid. We're afraid to lose, afraid of letting down our team and we're afraid of looking bad in front of our friends and family. John McEnroe, in his autobiography You Cannot Be Serious, admitted that his intense fear of losing outweighed his love of winning and often fueled his emotional rages. Sometimes, we're even afraid to win, because if we win we may be expected to win again, and who needs that kind of pressure?

Once the choking begins it can be like a recurring nightmare. Two years after her devastating loss to Graf, Novotna found herself with an even bigger lead in the third round of the 1995 French Open. Up 5-0 in the third set against American Chanda Rubin, Novotna's Devil undoubtedly whispered in her ear, "Remember Wimbledon?" She lost the match.

Racket rage

You're standing on the court, racket raised above your head, teeth clenched, muscles tense, a primal scream stirring in your belly. You've missed your third consecutive sitter, and the urge to slam dunk your racket into the court is overwhelming.

Anger is the enemy of every tennis player. Broken rackets, balls slammed into fences and over it, and a @#* vocabulary are a few of the most popular responses when our temper gets the better of us.

As the errors pile up, the anger increases and the vicious cycle continues, until we've missed enough shots to lose the match—or break all of our rackets forcing a default, as happened to touring pro Goran Ivanisevic a few years ago.

While John McEnroe and Jimmy Connors were known for being able to make their rage work for them, most of us don't have that ability. Though anger can sometimes help wake us up when our concentration falters, most of the time, as our temperatures rise, our level of play falls.

Though it is human nature for us to get nervous or angry during the heat of a match, the negative thoughts that accompany these emotions seldom bring positive results, so we need to learn to push them aside and get back on a positive path. The key lies with our inner voice.

Taming that voice inside our heads

Did you know that the average person talks to himself, verbally or non-verbally, approximately 50,000 times per day? Or, put another way, every two seconds of our lives we're telling ourselves something. Applying that information to our tennis lives during the average 90-minute, three-set match, we send ourselves a little over

3,000 messages and, for some, those messages are largely negative.

"My serve stinks."

"I move like an elephant."

"I can't believe I'm losing to her. I'm horrible!"

Here a few strategies to help you push the bad thoughts aside, keep your emotions in check and relieve some of the inevitable stress that comes with competition.

1. Become aware of your thoughts. Pay attention to the messages you're sending yourself. Keep a small notebook with you and, over several days, write down all your negative thoughts. You'll then be able to see how many times you put yourself down.

2. Break the pattern. When you feel the negative thoughts creeping in, take a deep breath and immediately say, "No! I am not going to do this." It sounds simplistic but it works.

3. Be positive. Stop the flow of negativity with a few positive, constructive statements. For example: Instead of telling yourself how slow or lazy you are, try saying something like, "Come on, you can get to those. Get up on your toes and run for every ball until it bounces twice." Or, after an unforced error remind yourself to "keep your eyes on the ball." Positive thoughts are vital. If you say it enough, you will believe it.

4. Observe your actions without judging them. This means being aware of what's happening on the court. For example, if you've hit your last three serves into the net, rather than getting upset, remind yourself that you have a tendency

to drop your head as you serve. Make the correction, tell yourself that you've "got it now," and move on to the next point.

Dr. John F. Murray, author of Smart Tennis (More info: johnfmurray.com), has devised a great experiment to help us monitor our self-talk. The next time you walk onto the court, place 40 paperclips in your right pocket. Each time you catch yourself making a negative comment to yourself, reach into your pocket and transfer one paperclip to the left pocket. At the end of the match see how many clips have gone to the left side. You might be shocked—and motivated to change.

Work at it and, slowly but surely, you'll see a change in the way you speak to yourself and, in turn, in the way you feel about yourself. After a month or two try the paperclip experiment again and see how you've improved.

Virtually no one plays well when they lose control of themselves so, even if you've made six unforced errors in a row and blown a four-game lead, keep your emotions under control. Push aside your desire to demonstrate your vast knowledge of obscenities and the urge to launch your racket into the parking lot. Take a few deep breaths, repeat some constructive, positive phrases to yourself and move on.

In a recent issue of Tennis magazine, trainer Pat Etcheberry (More info: etcheberryexperience.com) described a relaxation exercise in which he has his students play points with a potato chip in their mouths with the goal of not letting the chip break. "This drill makes it obvious when you're tensing up in your neck and face," says Etcheberry.

By becoming a more patient player and learning to control your emotions you'll significantly cut down on your number of unforced errors and will, in turn, stop being your own toughest opponent.

Jana Novotna did it. After her devastating losses to Graf and Rubin, she fought back, defeated her Tennis Devil and on July 5, 1998, raised the Champion's plate at Wimbledon.

Chapter 13

Don't Worry About The Opponent...Yet

W hile limiting your unforced errors and keeping the ball in play should always be your number one strategic approach, as you move beyond the 3.5 level, you're going to find that you'll need to take your strategy to the next level and understand the theories of high percentage tennis.

High percentage tennis means hitting the right shot at the right time. It means hitting the shot that gives you the least chance of committing an error while, at the same time, the best chance of staying in, or winning the point.

A tennis match between players of equal ability is a contest of patience, and it is the player, or team, who can be the more patient, executing high percentage shots, who will usually walk off the court the winner.

High percentage singles

What are those high percentage shots? Let's take a look at singles first. In its simplest form, the strategy for high percentages singles is as follows:

1. Never hit a second serve
2. Get every return of serve back in play
3. Hit your groundstrokes crosscourt.
4. Approach straight ahead.
5. Take control of the net.
6. When in doubt, throw it up

Never hit a second serve

When you have to hit a second serve you put yourself under a tremendous amount of stress because if you miss it, you lose the point. You also let your opponent know that your second serve is weaker than your first, so she moves up a few steps and is ready to attack. Take the second serve out of your game by getting your first serve in 80-90 percent of the time.

I believe successful tennis is a game of consistency and taking advantage of the proper percentages.—Bjorn Borg, five-time Wimbledon and six-time French Open champion

To do this, replace those big bomb first serve faults with medium-paced spin. The added control that spin provides will mean that you'll be able to get a higher percentage of first serves in the court and, from a psychological standpoint, that's a huge advantage, particularly on big points.

The next time you play a practice match, take away the security blanket of the second serve. Play sets where you only get one serve and before you know it, you'll find a medium-paced serve that you can put in the court every time.

> *I believe successful tennis is a game of consistency and taking advantage of the proper percentages.*
>
> Bjorn Borg
> Five-time Wimbledon and six-time French Open champion

Get every return of serve back in play

The serving player has the advantage on the first serve, but that advantage often shifts to the receiver on the second. Against a strong server, use their pace and simply block their first serve back. Aim five to seven feet above the net, down the middle of the court. If he follows his serve to the net, as many strong players will, aim one to two feet over the net and block it down at his feet.

If the server misses his first serve, shift into attack mode. Move three feet forward and, if your forehand is your favorite shot, two steps to the left. This will tell the server that you're going to hit your strongest shot after they hit their weakest serve. Step into the ball and drive a deep crosscourt return. Don't go for an outright winner, but rather a forcing shot where you can begin to dictate play.

Depending upon the quality of your opponent's second serve, you may be able to move forward and attack the net. If so, think of your return as an approach shot. Hit it straight ahead and move into the net.

Cross-court is king

During a match, 80-90 percent of your groundstrokes should be hit crosscourt. This is the highest percentage play for several reasons. First, the ball travels over the lowest part of the net at the center and second, the court is longer on the crosscourt diagonal than it is in a straight line. This means that you can hit the ball farther and still keep it in play.

In addition, by hitting crosscourt, you can make your opponent run farther than if you hit down the line. To illustrate this point, the next time you go out to practice, try this drill: As you and your practice partner rally, have one player hit all of his shots crosscourt while the other hits only down the line.

Once you get into a rhythm, you'll see that the person hitting only down the line is doing much more running than the player hitting crosscourt. Not only does this illustrate the point, it's also a great consistency and conditioning exercise.

Finally, when you hit crosscourt, you won't give your opponent as easy an angle to hit you off the court as you might if you hit down the line.

By keeping the ball consistently crosscourt, you're waiting for one of three mistakes from your opponent: an impatient error that gives you the point; a down-the-line shot that then allows you to drive the ball crosscourt and run them off the court; or a short ball that you can to attack with an approach shot.

Approach straight ahead

There's an old saying in singles that the point doesn't really begin until one player hits a short ball. When that short ball comes, the percentage play is to hit your approach shot straight ahead of where you strike the ball. You'll get the ball back to your opponent quicker since the ball is traveling on a straight line as opposed to the longer, crosscourt distance. Also, by approaching straight ahead, you simply move forward and are in the best position to cover your opponent's likely passing shots.

Finally, from a psychological standpoint, when you approach straight ahead, you'll always be in your opponent's line of vision as they move to hit their passing shot, adding a bit more pressure to their preparation. If you hit crosscourt, he'll be looking at a wide open court in front of him, at least until you are able to get across the court into the proper position.

Take control of the net

Even in this day of high-powered groundstrokes, the player that controls the net controls the point, so look for every opportunity to move forward and stake your claim to the net.

Keep in mind that just as patience wins from the backcourt, it's also a weapon at the net. Rarely will your first volley be one that you can end the point with, so be prepared to hit at least two volleys. Play the first one back deep. After that you can begin to look for a volley to put away.

Pick one that is above the net and that you can close in on. All the pressure is on your opponent when you're at the net, so don't force anything. If it takes four or five volleys and a few overheads to win the point, so be it.

When in doubt, throw it up

Yes, this is repetitive but repetition is the key to mastery. Many players, when put under pressure, will try to go for the big, crowd-pleasing, once-in-a-lifetime winner. You should know by now that that approach usually results in an error.

High-level players recognize when they're out of position, either relative to the ball or court, and rather than give their opponent a likely free point by trying a low percentage shot, they'll simply hit the ball back high and deep. They are, in a way, starting the point over, saying to their opponent, "I don't like this one, take it back and give me another." Remember, when in doubt, throw up a lob.

Percentage doubles

One of my students recently described a doubles match she'd seen between ladies at the 4.5 level. She said that she "couldn't believe how long their points lasted." She was further astonished that "the advantage would shift from team to team, sometimes three or four times during the course of the point." She finished by asking, "How do they do it?"

The players obviously understood the high percentage strategies of doubles. Good doubles should be a strategic battle with long points, exciting exchanges at the net and lots of twists and turns. To give your team an immediate advantage the next time you step on the court, remember the following:

1.   The team that controls the net usually wins the match.
2.   The team that hits the most clean winners usually losses the match.

On your mark, get set...go!

Good doubles is a race to the net and the team that wins that race will usually capture the match. Though control of the net is important in singles, it's even more of an advantage in doubles because proportionally each player has less space to cover.

When you take the net in singles you have to patrol 27 feet of court, sideline to sideline. In doubles, though the court is 9 feet wider due to the alleys you now have a partner to help you blanket that area. With each player responsible for covering only 18 feet of court, covering the net becomes much easier.

In addition, when your team stakes its claim to the net you put your opponents in a do or die situation: they have to come up with a forcing shot or you're in position to win the point with a volley or overhead.

California teaching professional Ken DeHart jokes that "controlling the net in doubles isn't that important...only the good teams do it." Dehart, one of only six teaching professionals in the world to have earned a Master Professional rating by both the PTR and USPTA, adds that "controlling the net is simply a matter of time management. When you take the net, you take away your opponent's time."

However, there is a catch: to be successful at the net, you and your partner must be able to cover the court properly, volley well, anticipate lobs from your opponents and hit solid overheads. Players below the 3.5 level who have yet to develop these skills are, understandably, reluctant to come to the net and frequently resort to the one up, one back formation that dominates the club scene.

Lower-level players will often say to me, "I take the backcourt, my partner plays the net and we've got it all covered." Actually, of the three basic formations at each team's disposal—one player up and one back, two at the net, or two at the baseline—this popular formation is the least desirable.

First, in this setup, there's a huge gap between the two players into which their opponents can hit. Second, if the other team's players both come to the net, the single player at the net becomes a sitting duck.

If the other team wins the sprint to the net, you're often better off having both players move back to the baseline. Though it is a defensive position, you won't give your opponents a mid-court target and you'll be surprised how long you can stay in, and often turn around, the point by mixing up drives and lobs.

High-level doubles players hang out at the net, so tighten your tennis shoes, grab your partner by their wristband and get ready to sprint to a more winning style of doubles.

Clean winners are for doubles losers

"Hit 'em where they ain't"

These were the words most of us heard during our first introduction to tennis strategy. Translation: Hit to the open space so that your opponent won't be able to touch the ball and you'll win the point. While this is reasonable advice when playing singles, for those who play doubles on a regular basis, it's a poor percentage play.

A good doubles team will consistently shift from side to side following the ball and position themselves so that the only "open" space on the court is the spot that's most difficult for your team to hit.

With that in mind, I tell my doubles players to stay away from the "hit 'em where they ain't" approach. Let the other team go for the clean winners. They'll hit a few, but over the course of a long match they'll miss far more than they'll make. They can have their clean winners while you and your partner win the match.

The vast majority of points won in high-level doubles are won by hitting to three places:

1. Down the middle.
2. At your opponents' feet.
3. Over their heads.

Down the middle

This is always a good shot in doubles for many reasons. First, a shot hit down the middle of the court travels over the lowest part of the net giving you more margin for error. When you hit down the middle, there will always be an element of confusion for your opponents over whose ball it is. How often have you and your partner turned and given each other the "where were you look" as the ball went untouched between the two of you?

In addition, if you hit to the outsides of the court, you give your opponents the opportunity to angle the ball away for a winner. When you play down the center, they have to create their own angle, which is a difficult thing to do. Finally, if you hit down the center and don't hit the ball well, you'll probably still keep it in play. If you aim for the alleys or the outsides of the court and miss your target, you'll most likely hit the ball out.

Vic Braden says, "I've long been fascinated by the intermediates who say, 'Watch your alley,' while the pros are always talking about protecting the middle. Intermediates are so afraid of their opponents hitting down the line that one of them plays wide to the left and the other wide to the right. Unfortunately, they're one man short. They're so intent on guarding their alleys that when a ball is hit down the middle, they both automatically turn and say, 'Yours!' You always want to entice your opponents to try those difficult, low percentage shots to your outside." Well said, Vic!

At their feet

This is a difficult concept for many players to accept, because it is the exact opposite approach of "hit 'em where they ain't." However, in a competitive situation, quite often the best strategy is a shot hit right at your opponent. I can't tell you how many times I've seen a player with an easy, high volley make an error because, trying to keep the ball away from his opponent, he angled the ball off the court instead of simply hitting right down at his opponent's feet.

Obviously, you're not trying to hit the opposing player, but rather aim the ball at him in such an awkward location that he'll struggle to get it back. Even if he does manage to return the ball, he'll have to hit "up" because your shot is so low. Most likely you'll get an easy sitter to put away either down the middle or right back at his feet.

A brief word about hitting the opposing player: It's not the nicest thing to say, but more often than not, when players get hit, it's their own fault. They're either in the wrong position or not paying attention. Good doubles is a fast, aggressive game where the best shot is often right at your opponent. It's up to all players to make sure that

"Where were you?"

they stay alert, are positioned properly and protect themselves. In a competitive match, if you do accidentally hit someone, immediately make sure that he's not hurt, offer him a minute to compose himself and, in the spirit of good sportsmanship, apologize—but don't hesitate to go right back at him if the opportunity presents itself again.

Over their heads

Lob again? Yes! The lob is one the most aggressive shots in the game. Be it the high, deep defensive lob that gives you time to recover or the low, offensive lob used to surprise your opponents and win the point outright, every good player possesses and understands the benefits of an effective lob.

Play the percentages

When you step on the doubles court make a mental shift in your shot selection from thinking side to side, as you do in singles, to low or high. Hit the ball at your opponents' feet to force them to pop it up, or hit it high over their heads so you can take the net away from them.

If your opponents have control of the net and you are not certain you can get the ball down low, put it up in the air. Force them to move back and hit another shot. Make your opponents hit the ball to beat you rather than beating yourself with an unnecessary error.

Hit the ball down the middle, at their feet, or over their heads. Select your shots with these tips in mind and watch your errors decrease and you number of wins increase.

Percentage tennis is a systematic approach to strategy that will be effective against every opponent you face. I've summarized these percentages in Table 13.1 below. Tear out this small section of the book, put it in your racket bag and look at it before each match. Remind yourself that percentage tennis is winning tennis!

Table 13-1

Singles	Doubles
Never hit a second serve.	The team that controls the net controls the match.
Get every return of serve back in play.	Let your opponents go for the "clean" winner.
Hit your groundstrokes crosscourt.	Down the middle.
Hit your approach shots straight ahead.	At their feet.
Get to the net.	Over their heads.
Lob	Lob

A DIFFERENT TYPE OF PERCENTAGE PLAY

If you win the toss, let your opponent serve first. It constantly amazes me how players reflexively elect to serve when they win the toss. When I ask my students why they make this choice they think for a moment and then say, "It's an advantage to serve first...isn't it?"

The pros almost always elect to serve first. The serve is the most important shot in the game and most professionals have a good one, so for them the decision is a no-brainer. However, if you're like me, you're not receiving a check for your match results so the subject requires a bit more thought.

Serving first is theoretically the right choice because serving is an advantage—theoretically. But realistically is it the correct decision? I say, most of the time, "No!"

Serving at the recreational level is often a disadvantage for the simple fact that many recreational players do not have particularly good serves. To anyone
insulted by that statement, I apologize but, hey, we're talking competitive tennis here and, more often than not, serving first does not give you an advantage.

The pros tend to hold serve (win their service games) about 85 percent of the time. At the recreational levels I estimate the percentages are approximately as follows:

> 1.0-2.0: 20%
> 2.0-3.0: 30%
> 3.0-4.0: 40%
> 4.0-4.5: 50%
> 4.5-5.5: 60%

As you can see, until you reach the 4.5-5.0 level serving tends to be a risky affair at best. That is why I suggest you choose to receive serve if you win the opening spin of the racket.

Here are a few reasons why:

1. You'll catch your opponent cold. Like most recreational players, they've probably hit three or four serves and then boldly proclaim that they're ready to go. Believe me, they're not! They'll undoubtedly still be a bit stiff, as well as suffering from opening game jitters.

   In social tennis, there's often the old "first ball in" (FBI) rule in effect, meaning that on the first point the server gets to keep hitting serves until they get one in. This concept was invented for one reason: so that the players don't have to waste valuable court time on something as insignificant as warming up their serves.

   So what happens? The player serving first takes no warm-up serves, says "FBI" and away they go. Many times in FBI games the first ball actually does go in and then the server's really in trouble. They now have to serve the rest of the game with what amounts to only one warm-up serve.

   A quick point here: If you do get caught in one of those "first ball in" games be certain to intentionally miss your first 10-15 serves so that you can loosen your arm up. By doing so, you'll not only warm your arm up, you'll most probably annoy your opponents to the point where they'll agree to a proper service warm-up before beginning the match.

2. You'll have more time to warm-up, relax and get into the match. In addition, you'll be looser when it's your turn to serve.

3. Most players below the 5.0 level simply don't have very good serves. Sorry, but it's true. Many players at the club level find practicing their serve boring so they let it slide. As a result, they adopt the old "boom" and "plop" strategy that is so prevalent today.

   Of course there are exceptions to the rule. If you have confidence in your serve, and I don't mean the "I have a great serve when it goes in" type of confidence, then you should consider serving first. Also, if your opponent truly has a great serve you may want to serve first. However, keep in mind that even a great server is a bit stiff and jittery serving for the first time, so it may be a good time to go for an early service break.

Chapter 14

Customizing Your Gameplan

When Jimmy Connors walked onto the court for the 1975 Wimbledon final he was the undisputed king of the tennis world. Twenty-two years old, Connors was the defending Wimbledon and U.S. Open champion and hadn't lost a set in the tournament. His opponent was 31-year-old Arthur Ashe. Ashe's career was on the decline and London bookmakers had made him a 5-1 underdog. Many insiders felt he would do well to win a set.

Connors won the first game of the match. Ashe won 12 of the next 13 and a short while later became the first black man to win Wimbledon. Ashe's 6-1, 6-1, 5-7, 6-4 victory is still considered one of the greatest upsets in tennis history.

The night before the final, Ashe and a few of his friends got together over dinner and came up with a game plan to defeat Connors. They made a list of five or six things for Arthur to focus on during the match. Ashe took this list to the court, referred to it during changeovers and took out the "unbeatable" Connors in four sets.

Whether your strategy is simply to keep the ball in play while waiting for an error or something more complex, learning to analyze your competition and putting together a game-plan are vital ingredients in achieving victory against players at the 4.0 level and above.

It begins with the warm-up

Beginning with the warm up and continuing throughout the match, you should be gathering information on your opponent's strengths, weaknesses and tendencies. Feed a ball right at her body and see which stroke she chooses to hit. This might tell you whether she prefers her forehand or backhand—an important piece of information

As you're hitting back and forth, take note of things such as:

1. Is she right or left-handed? Believe it or not, many players don't notice this until they're told after the match.

2. What kind of forehand grip does she use? Every grip in the game has its advantages and disadvantages. For example, if she uses the Semi-Western or Western grip, she'll have a tough time with low balls. If she uses a Continental grip, high bouncing balls will give her fits.

3. Does she hit a one or two-handed backhand? If she's using a two hander, she may be able to generate more pace and topspin, but wide balls will give her trouble, as will low shots and balls hit above her head. If she has a one-handed backhand, she may have trouble generating topspin and will also struggle with balls hit shoulder height or above.

4. Does she seem to hit with excessive topspin or slice?

Give her a variety of shots: high, low, soft, hard and see how she reacts. Does she hustle after the ball or does she let it bounce twice. How well does she bend for low balls? How about moving back for an overhead? Does she seem relaxed or uptight? Does she get angry at herself over missed shots? Pay attention to all of these and begin to get a feel for her game and temperament.

If you're playing doubles, take note of these same things with each player on the opposing team, but also try to see which member of the team appears to be the leader. The leader is often the stronger player and knowing that right off the bat will give your team a big advantage. When you spin the racket, see which member of the team calls "up or down" and makes the decision whether to serve or receive. That player may very well be the leader.

A final word about the warm-up

Don't be too concerned if, during the warm-up, it seems as if you're on the court with Andy Roddick. Many players, in an attempt to get the upper hand will start hitting big shots right off the bat. They hope that by "winning the warm-up" they'll intimidate you when the "real" match begins.

Don't panic. You're not playing Andy Roddick and I can assure you that these "win-the- warm-up" players won't be quite as smooth and loose once the score is being kept.

Start off like a backboard and play the percentages

During the first two or three games, keep the ball in play and focus on playing classic "percentage" tennis. By hitting a lot of balls during the first few games, you can continue to check out your opponent as well as settle into a comfortable rhythm. As the match progresses and you learn more and more about your opponent's skills, both technically and strategically, you can begin to make them work for you.

Singles: Here are 10 things you might notice in your opponent and how to use them to your advantage:

Table 14-1

Opponent's Skills & Strategies	Make it work for you by
Western grip forehand.	Using slice and forcing him to hit low shots.
Two-handed backhand.	Jamming him with balls into his body and making him stretch for balls out wide.
Loses patience after three shots.	Hitting medium-paced, high balls down the center of the court.
Can rally from the baseline all day long.	Taking him out of his comfort zone and coming to the net.
Returns all balls above his chest with a lob.	Rolling a high groundstroke to the backhand corner and then moving up toward the net.
Weak second serve.	Hitting straight ahead and attacking the net.
Moves up and back poorly.	Drawing him in with a short ball or drop shot and then lob.
Drives all backhand passing shots cross-court.	Just before he makes contact, taking two steps forward and to the side to cover the crosscourt pass. Volley to the open court.

Big hitter from both sides.	Making him generate his own pace by hitting deep, high, soft shots.
Is a much stronger player in every aspect of the game.	Not panicking and going for shots you don't own. Get lots of balls back in play, come to the net and make him prove he's better.

When playing **doubles**, look for:

Table 14-2

Opposing Team's Strengths & Weaknesses	Make it work for you by
Very strong serve and volley players.	Lobbing the return of serve over the server's partner.
Opposing team plays the one up, one back formation.	Taking control of the net and volleying between the two players or down at the opposing net players feet.
One team member is decidedly weaker than the other.	Ganging up on him and play two against one. You and your partner hit virtually every shot towards the weak link.
They always lob.	Still coming to the net but stop at the service line so you can handle their lobs with overheads.
They never, ever lob.	Both you and your partner position yourselves three feet away from the net.

These are just a few examples of what to look for when you analyze your opponent's games. Become an aware player and pay attention to everything. The more information you can gather, the better you'll be able to devise your game plan. Many times you'll find, early on, that all you need to do is hit a few balls back in the court, use the percentage plays, and wait for your opponents to beat themselves.

However, as your game improves, tennis becomes much more of a strategic battle in which the thinking player will almost always come out on top. Knowing how to analyze and take advantage of your opponent's game is your first step towards winning matches at the higher levels.

Chapter 15

Making Your Opponent Sing Your Song

At the 4.5 level and beyond, the player that can impose his game plan most effectively will usually win the match. Just as the Dallas Cowboys and New York Knicks have a book of plays that they run during their games, you need to put together a mental playbook that you can use during your matches. These plays are called patterns.

Simply put, a pattern is a predetermined sequence of two or more shots that you combine to begin dictating the point. They can be used when serving, receiving and during rallies throughout every point you play. Here are a few patterns to try the next time you take the court against a tough opponent.

Serving Patterns

As you toss the ball have two shots planned: your serve and your response to your opponent's return. Here are three serving patterns that will be effective against any opponent:

- Serve out wide to pull your opponent off the court and then hit your second shot to the open court. This one's a favorite of Andre Agassi.
- Serve down the "T", pulling them towards the center of the court and then hit behind them.
- Serve right into their body and hit your second shot into the open court.

Return of Serve Patterns

Your goals when returning serve are to first, get the ball back in play and second, take away the server's advantage. To do so, focus on these three patterns.

- When facing a big serve, return the serve high over the net and down the middle of the court. Hit your second shot crosscourt.
- Against a serve and volley player, return low at their feet and then lob over their head.
- When returning a short or weak serve, hit your return straight ahead, move into the net and then hit your second shot -volley or overhead crosscourt.

A favorite pattern of mine is to hit a drop shot off my opponent's second serve. They seldom expect it, usually struggle to reach it and, more often than not, meekly pop it back over the net. I've then got an easy passing shot or I can torture them with a lob over their heads.

Never become so predictable in your serving patterns that your opponent knows ahead of time where the ball is coming, how fast and with what sort of spin.

Manuel Orantes
1975 U.S. Open champion

Baseline Patterns

As you and your opponent are exchanging groundstrokes, wait for a ball in your strike zone, step into your shot and take control of the point by using one of these patterns.

- Every ball crosscourt. This is the most basic of patterns in which you're trying to lure your opponent into losing their patience and trying a low percentage shot. You can stay in this pattern for an entire point or until you get a ball you can attack.

- Three shots crosscourt and then one down the line. After your opponent has seen three crosscourt shots in a row they'll subconsciously begin leaning crosscourt. When you drive the ball down the line, you'll often get them scrambling.
- Two shots to the forehand and then hit a high deep shot to the backhand. No player in the world likes to hit a high ball to their backhand so when you throw this shot in, immediately take a step or two forward to anticipate a weak return.

Another favorite of mine is that when I find myself trading backhands with my opponent, I like to hit three deep crosscourt shots and then throw in a down-the-line drop shot. As they scramble forward to get it, I've already got my point-ending lob planned.

Doubles Patterns

Few things feel better in doubles than when you and your partner execute a patterned play to perfection.

When your team is serving:

- Serve down the middle, follow your serve to the net, and hit your first volley cross-court, putting you and your partner in a commanding net position.
- Serve down the middle; your partner poaches and puts the volley away at the opposing net player's feet.
- Serve out wide; your partner fakes a poach to draw a down-the-alley return, which he then volleys between your two opponents.

When your team is receiving:

- Lob over the net players head, attack the net with your partner and then hit your volley or overhead between your two opponents.
- Against a serve and volley team, hit the return at their feet; your partner poaches and then volleys down the middle.
- If the server stays back, drive a deep return crosscourt, join your partner at the net and hit your first volley crosscourt.

BIG HITTERS AND PUSHERS
Two playing styles that strike fear into the eyes of the recreational player

Big hitters are the ones who draw the "oohs" and "aahs" from the crowd. Their goal is to hit winners, and they've never seen a ball they couldn't hit back harder. They look good even when they miss, because their shots outrun the radar gun and sound so impressive.

The pusher is the opposite of the big hitter. Pushers hardly ever try to hit winners. They do nothing with the ball except lob it back down the middle of the court, usually without much pace, and wait for you to miss.

We've all faced these types of players, and often our first reaction is to panic. We get nervous, rush our shots and feel inadequate because our games aren't as impressive looking as that of the big hitter or as steady as that of the pusher. Fortunately, by reaching into our playbook, we can pull out some winning patterns to send them both packing.

The big hitter

Big hitters are usually impatient, seldom consistent players. If you can put a few balls back into play, more often than not, they'll hit themselves right out of the match. The next time you find yourself across the net from a big hitter, try these two simple patterns:

- Take the pace off your shots and hit three soft, high, deep balls to his backhand side. On the third shot, charge the net.
- Big hitters need the ball in their strike zone, so alternate high and low groundstrokes. After four shots, throw in a drop shot.

The pusher

The pusher is counting on you to lose your cool by continuously floating the ball back over the net. You can turn the tables on him by taking him out of his comfort zone. Here are two patterns that will do the trick:

- Most pushers aren't comfortable at the net. After hitting two groundstrokes, pull the "pusher" into the net with a short slice or drop shot, and then either pass him or force him to hit a difficult volley.
- Try a sneak attack. Hit three high, deep balls and then quickly move forward and take the pusher's next ball out of the air and move up to the net. The pusher will now have to come up with a quality shot or you'll be in position to end the point.

Stay away from bad patterns

As you try to impose your patterns of play onto your opponent, he'll undoubtedly be doing the same. Learn to recognize your opponent's patterns and try to break them. For example, my forehand is my weakest shot. Everyone I play against knows it and does their best to get me in a crosscourt forehand exchange during the point.

Knowing my weakness, as soon as I recognize my opponent moving into a forehand-to- forehand pattern, I immediately break it by hitting a high ball down the line to their backhand. They usually return the ball crosscourt to my backhand, at which point I can begin to work my backhand to backhand pattern—my favorite.

Patterns are your game plan for victory

The number of patterns you can come up with are endless. While you're in front of the television, daydreaming at your desk, or waiting in traffic, think of some creative shot combinations. Take them to the court with you and give them a try.

By coming up with two or three simple patterns from each area of the court and learning to execute them well, you'll often be able to dictate play and ultimately move in for the kill.

Tennis has frequently been compared to chess and the description is well deserved. By following patterns and imposing your strategies you'll be well on your way to checkmating your opponent.

Chapter 16

Take The Court
With Tony Robbins

Anthony Robbins is one of the world's foremost success coaches. He's written five books, created Personal Power, the No.1 personal and professional development system of all time (More info: anthonyrobbins.com) and has worked with world leaders, major corporations and professional athletes such as Andre Agassi and Greg Norman. An expert in time management, Robbins trains his clients to break time down into distinct periods and teaches them to take control of each period and use it to their advantage.

Tennis matches are made up of three distinct time periods: points, between points and changeovers. Taking Tony's advice and developing a strategy for each of these time periods will go a long way toward helping you win more matches

During the point

Paul Fein, in his brilliant book Tennis Confidential, wrote that in the 1991 Wimbledon final in which Michael Stich defeated Boris Becker, "the ball was actually in play for nine minutes and twenty seconds in the two and a half hour match."

> *The bad news is time flies. The good news is you're the pilot.*
>
> Michael Altshuler

Granted the match was played on grass and Stich and Becker were two of the games biggest hitters but the fact remains that, during most tennis matches, the ball is actually in play less than 25 percent of the time.

When you're in the middle of a point, you're running, stretching, hitting and trying to gain the advantage. You don't have time to think. Let the training and drilling you've done in practice take over. Focus on preparing early and hitting the ball cleanly to your targets. Keep your feet moving and patiently execute your patterns while waiting for an opportunity to take control of the point.

To help yourself stay calm and maintain your patience when the ball's in play, come up with a mantra that you can recite to yourself. When I play matches, I'm constantly reciting the words "deep and smart" to myself as the ball moves back and forth across the net.

This simple phrase keeps me calm and reminds me to focus on hitting my shots deep and to play smart/percentage tennis. Find your own mantra and recite it to yourself during your points.

In-between points

The point has ended and you now have 25 seconds to get ready for the next. Tennis points can be extremely long and strenuous so when the point ends, you need to first catch your breath and come down from the emotional stress of the point. Turn away from your opponent and walk to the back fence.

Your mind dwells on where your eyes focus so resist the urge to look around. Keep your vision within the confines of the court. Place your racket in your left hand and look down at your strings. Take 4-5 deep, controlled breaths and, as you push the air out, relax your neck and shoulders. Give yourself 5-10 seconds to recover.

After you've caught your breath, take the next 5-10 seconds to relive the previous point. Observe, without emotion, why you won or lost the point. Give yourself two quick tips and then move on. For example, if your opponent beat you to the net and hit a winning volley, remind yourself to "aim higher over the net to keep the ball deep." If she made an error on her backhand side, remind yourself to "keep pounding the backhand." Keep it brief and simple, you don't have time for in-depth strategizing.

With the remaining few seconds you need to gear yourself up for the next point. Bounce up and down on your toes. Take a long look at your opponent and give yourself a quick tip for your next shot. If you're serving, visualize where you'll place your serve. Say to yourself, "out wide" or "into the body." If you're receiving serve, tell yourself to "focus on the ball and block it back."

The changeover

During the changeover you have 90 seconds before the next game begins. Andre Agassi sprints to his chair as soon as the changeover begins. You should get there quickly as well. Like a boxer between rounds, sit down, towel off your arms, legs and neck. Sip your water, close your eyes and take five deep breaths. Use the first 20 seconds to physically and emotionally recover from the previous two games.

Over the next 45 seconds, take a good look at what's happening at this point in the match. Review the last two games and pay attention to how you're winning and losing points. If your forehand's letting you down, figure out patterns that will bring more balls to your backhand.

If you notice that your opponent's backhand is landing short in the court, plan a pattern that gets the ball to their backhand side. If you're tiring, tell yourself to shorten the points by coming to the net.

"His backhand's weak... attack it!"

During the changeover also be sure to take note of your opponent's body language. Does he appear to be getting angry, frustrated or tired? If the answer is yes, you're obviously getting to him, so stick with the patterns you've been using.

Most players will hit the same shots again and again in a given situation so remind yourself of your opponent's tendencies. Where does he serve on big points? When you attack the net on his forehand side, does he try to pass you crosscourt or down the line? Recognizing and reacting to these tendencies can often win you the match.

I saw a great example of this recently when two players, Bill and John, faced each other in their club championship finals. Throughout the match, Bill paid strict attention to John's patterns and noticed that on big points John hit his backhand passing shots crosscourt.

When the third set tiebreaker reached six points all, John had an easy backhand passing shot to win the match. Bill remembered his crosscourt tendency and, just before John struck the ball, he moved to cover the crosscourt shot. John stayed true to form, and Bill had an easy put away.

Two points later, the same situation presented itself, only this time Bill held the match point. Again, John ripped his passing shot crosscourt and again Bill anticipated correctly and won the point—and the match. That little piece of information Bill picked up, and had actually written down during a changeover, won him the title.

Finally, you need to plan your strategy for the next two games. If you're winning the match, don't change a thing. As the legendary Bill Tilden once said, "Never change a winning game." If you're comfortably ahead or the match is close, stick with your game plan. Bounce up out of your chair and be the first back on the court. Let your opponent see that you're eager to play.

If you find yourself slightly behind, don't panic. Close matches are usually decided by a few points. Stick with your game plan. If you can win a few of those big points, you can easily turn the match in your favor.

If you're getting blown off the court, slow the pace of the match down. Use every one of your 90 seconds. Let your opponent walk back onto the court first. Make him wait for you. Once play resumes, use the full 25 seconds between points.

Just because your opponent may be on a hot streak for the first few games of the match, it doesn't mean that he can keep it up for the full two or three sets. By making him play to your pace, within the rules, of course, you can often take him out of his rhythm and turn the match around.

Seventy-five percent of a tennis match is spent not hitting the ball, and the winner is usually the player who can more effectively devise, adjust and execute their strategy. If you can learn to win this "game within the game," you'll most likely be the one smiling at the end of the match.

Chapter 17

Win Or Lose,
You Always Learn

The match is over and now it's time to learn from the experience. There are two ways to analyze your performance after your matches: self-analysis, during which you'll gauge your physical and emotional response to the match, and a videotape analysis during which you can check out your strokes and strategy. By using both you'll get a complete picture of your game and what you need to do to bring it to the next level.

Get in touch with your feelings

Your main goal with a self-analysis is to take a look at how you reacted physically and emotionally to the pressure of the match.

If you found that you tired during long points, you'll need to increase your stamina. Side- to-side hitting drills are great for improving your endurance as are off-court activities like biking, rollerblading and fast walking. Your body already takes a lot of pounding during your matches so keep running to a minimum. If you're forced inside, head for the Stairmaster, elliptical trainer or treadmill.

Something I tried recently and which I found to be both great exercise and lots of fun is Aqua jogging (More info: aquajogger.com). As you can probably guess from its name, Aqua jogging is done in a pool with a special vest that keeps you buoyant. Your legs are working against the water's resistance so they're getting a great workout without suffering any pounding. Start off by jogging in place for two minutes and then increase as your endurance improves.

If you felt slow getting to the ball, you need to increase your speed, and that means sprints. Andre Agassi sprints up a hill near his home in Las Vegas. You can do the same or, to lessen the stress, set a treadmill at an incline to do your sprint work.

Donald Chu, in his book Power Tennis Training outlines an entire program of tennis exercise designed to improve your speed and endurance.

How did you handle the pressure?

When the big points arrived, how did you respond? Did you rise to the occasion or did you choke? If your nerves got the better of you when it counted most, you need to recreate that pressure when you play your practice matches.

A great way to simulate match pressure is to play practice sets with specific scoring situations. Here are two of my favorites:

1. Play a set where each player gets only one serve and each game begins at 30-40. Having to hit a second serve on break point is one of the greatest pressures we'll face during our matches. This drill will help you learn to deal with that pressure.

2. Play a set in which the winner of each game gets a point advantage in the next game. If your practice partner is serving and wins the first game, you serve the second down 0-15. If you lose that game, your practice partner then serves the third game with a lead of 30-0.

If you then lose that game, you're down 0-40 in the next. If you drop that game you continue on to the next game down 0-40. If you fight back and win that game you then serve with a lead of 15-0, and so on. It's a great exercise that teaches you how to fight from behind.

Recording your match

Even the most aware players are limited to what they can pick up and retain during their matches, so it's great to have a record of the match that you can go back and refer to.

Videotaping and charting are two ways to record your match. I prefer videotaping over charting for the simple reason that you can do it by yourself. However, charting can be fun and educational when you watch team members or the pros play matches. At the end of the book, I've included a very basic chart that I use when watching my players compete (More info: Appendix E Unforced Errors). It's very user friendly and focuses on unforced errors—the enemy of us all.

There's also a great computer software program for charting matches on the market. It's called Ace Tennis Match and can analyze 200 statistics in 8 different categories.

There's no hiding from the camera

Using a tripod, set the camera behind and above the court. If that's not possible, shoot through the back fence. You want to be sure that the camera captures the entire court so that you can see how you move and react from all areas, as well as how you respond to your opponent's position.

When you sit down to watch the tape, disassociate yourself from the player on the screen and play the part of tennis analyst. What do you see? Take a look at your

"You served to his forehand everytime."

strokes, your shot patterns and note what's working and what isn't. I can promise you that you'll be surprised.

If possible, have your pro watch the video with you. An educated professional can point out specific areas of your game that you may not notice. You may find your strokes bear very little resemblance to how you picture them in your mind, and you'll better understand your pro's instructions when you can physically see what he's referring to.

If you play on a team, you'll probably have a pro working with you who attends your matches and will be available to watch your video. If not, expect to pay the pro for his time and expertise.

As you watch your match video, look for these four common errors:

1. Poor footwork: This leads to a breakdown of your stroke. If I had a dollar for every time I've told a player they're too close to the ball, I could buy Wimbledon.
2. Not completing your stroke: Under the pressure of a match, it's easy to get tentative and simply "bunt" the ball back over the net. Pay attention to your strokes and make sure that you're driving through all of your shots. Remember, hit through three balls.
3. Impatience: If you're off balance either relative to the ball—too close or far away—or the court—well behind the baseline or off to the side—don't try to end the point with a spectacular low-percentage winner. Lob the ball back and give your opponent another opportunity to make an error.
4. Predictability: It's amazing how often a player will serve to the same spot every single time and not be aware of it.

Whether you won or lost your last match, there is always something to be learned. As you move through your self-analysis and video analysis, keep in mind that the purpose of both is your improvement. Be honest with yourself and insist that your pro do the same. By absorbing all of the information you gathered, you'll be able to put together an on- and off-court plan to take your match play to the next level.

Part 4

Lighten Up, Be Happy

We all want to win more tennis matches and, by following the advice in Parts 1-3, I can guarantee that you will.

However, when all is said and done our time around the game should be one of the most enjoyable aspects of our lives. The words I treasure most from my students when they come off the court are, "Greg, that was so much fun! Tennis is one of the happiest parts of my week."

When you participate in the world of social tennis, unfortunately, all is not always strawberries and cream. There is a game within the game, and in this part of the book I'm going to help you chart a path through some of the more stressful, frustrating and sensitive issues that arise on the social tennis scene.

We'll take a look at why we play the game, and I'll show you how to thrive under the glare of the dreaded tennis snob.

You'll learn how to smooth out the bumpy situation of leaving your instructor for another, and you will see how we can be the kind of players everyone wants on their court.

Finally, a strategy that will allow you, and your children, to enjoy the game for years to come, as well as show you a new way of looking at your tennis that will make you feel like a winner each and every time you step onto the court.

Chapter 18

Finding Victory In Every Match

I play tennis because it feels good. I love the feeling of hitting a solid shot, and I revel in the exercise and exhaustion of a hard workout. I love the people, the laughs and the friendly competition. Most of all, I love the fact that, after 35 years on a tennis court, I'm still learning about the game and myself.

Why do you play? Exercise, camaraderie, competition? Whatever your reasons, tennis should be one of the highlights of your day. It should bring enjoyment to your life for the rest of your life.

Unfortunately, our path to a long life of enjoyable tennis is not a straight one, and we usually face more than a few bad bounces along the way. The happiness we derive from tennis is a direct result of the attitude we bring to it and the effort we put into it. Interestingly, both often change as our game improves.

A life in the game has shown me that our psychological evolution as tennis players is a three-stage process. Stage 1 begins when we are in our tennis infancy.

Stage 1: Just starting out

As a beginner, we're like a kid on Christmas morning. We're ecstatic to get a new racket with the wrapper still on the grip. We get pumped up with a brand new pair of tennis shoes and wear our "Tennis Anyone?" t-shirt with great pride. We're eager to learn and able to laugh at ourselves. We're just having fun and it's virtually impossible for us not to get better.

Unfortunately, this wonderful, wide-eyed approach to the game often fades as we begin to improve. We receive a few compliments about our play, the club pro pays us a little extra attention, and players who wouldn't even speak to us before are now asking us to join in their games.

Soon, our inner voice tells us how important it is to play well so that we can hang on to our newfound status. Our image as a tennis player is of the utmost concern, and the players we beat or lose to define our place in the club hierarchy.

The pressure is on, and the pure enjoyment of attempting to execute a proper stroke has been overcome by a crippling fear of failure. Our ego is on the line, and God forbid we should look bad in front of someone else. It seems that our climb up the tennis ladder often ignites our descent into tennis misery. Welcome to Stage 2!

Stage 2: It's all about the score

Comparisons, expectations and self-evaluations are our enemies when we reach Stage 2. We crave achievement, want instant improvement and constantly put ourselves under a microscope, comparing ourselves to others in order to gauge our progress. We've become fixated on the outcome, which either pumps up or deflates our egos. Each time on the court becomes a pressure-filled event, a test.

> *The players who have trouble enjoying themselves are players who constantly expect too much of themselves.*
>
> Rod Laver
> Two-time winner of the Grand Slam of tennis

Stage 2 robs us of our ability to see and be happy with ourselves as we are. We may play our best, yet still feel inadequate if the score says we lost. Not only does this increase our stress level it also greatly inhibits our willingness to learn.

Our pro may suggest a grip change or encourage us to develop a new shot but we resist because we may take a step or two backward. It takes time to develop a new skill and it's true that we'll often take a step or two backward while trying.

When we're in Stage 2, we feel that we can't afford to take that step back because we might look foolish or lose to someone we "shouldn't lose to." Our ego won't allow us to suffer through this learning phase and, as a result, our improvement stagnates and our frustration grows. When you find yourself trapped in Stage 2, and you will, the key to escape lies in recognizing the stress and the "what-ifs" when they begin to creep in.

Dr. Robert Heller, sports psychologist and certified teaching professional, says "by recognizing, and then changing, your perspective, you can achieve greater control over your thoughts and behaviors."

Heller, the author of the mental conditioning CD-ROM program, Tennis Mind (More info: thewinningedge.usptapro.com), says that "players need to separate their tennis performance from their self-worth and focus more on the thrill and challenge of competing and less on the winning or losing." He suggests the following mental exercise to "regain a healthy perspective during a match."

Following a point or at the changeover, envision yourself later on that day laughing with friends or enjoying time with your family.

> *If we focus too much on striving, we may forget what we're ultimately striving for—to feel good about ourselves, to experience happiness, to reach our highest human potential.*
>
> Dan Millman
> Author of The Inner Athlete

Remind yourself that tennis is just a game and that your

life will continue just fine regardless of any success or failure you may be experiencing at that moment."

Always remember that the ESPN truck is not parked outside the club waiting to report your latest loss. Your friends and family will still love you, even if you lose love and love!

When you feel the pressure beginning to build, take a deep breath, relax your shoulders and, above all, keep your sense of humor. When my students begin to "stress out," I can often bring them back by cracking a few jokes or even making fun of them in a good-natured way. Humor is a great antidote for stress.

Stage 3: Your ultimate destination

A while back, I was playing a practice match with Dan, a friend of mine. I was down match point. After a 20-shot exchange, Dan came to the net and I ripped a passing shot by him that landed just long. As Dan extended his index finger signaling that the ball was out, I remember thinking, "Boy, that point was fun!" It never occurred to me that I'd lost the match. When I realized that I'd just enjoyed the point that lost me the match, I knew I'd reached my ultimate goal as a tennis player—Stage 3.

When you reach Stage 3 you've come full circle back to Stage 1 from an emotional standpoint. You've learned to calm your mind and let go of the comparisons that dominated your thinking in Stage 2. You've gotten over the constant need to judge yourself and prove your worth as a tennis player.

You remember that the prize is the process. You still do everything possible to play your best, but now you approach tennis from a much different perspective. You realize that tennis is simply a game that's supposed to be a source of enjoyment, so you relax and embrace that enjoyment. With this enlightenment comes a type of liberation. Free of internal roadblocks, you're once again able to pursue the game with a passion.

In Stage 3, you develop a healthy selfishness. You view your game from a total inner standpoint. You observe your tennis without judging it and ask yourself questions such as, "Did I hit the ball well in my last match?" "Is my new topspin backhand coming along?" "How about that slice serve I've been working on?" "Am I playing at a higher level than I was six months ago?" You see your mistakes, take note of them and move on

Dr. George Sheehan, the late runner, author and philosopher, who also happened to be an avid tennis player writes that, "sport is not a test but a therapy, not a trial but a reward, not a question but an answer." He said we should not be "intimidated by the opinion of others," and should pursue our own perfection. This is Stage 3.

Don't judge your progress merely by the score of a match. Have a larger vision in which you assess your performance in terms of achieving certain goals that you set before you took the court. For example, the next time you step onto the court, set a goal of running harder than usual for each shot. Another goal might be to hit that topspin second serve that you've been practicing.

Stage 3 players realize that the outcome of a match can frequently have nothing to do with how well they played. Perhaps you played great, hit all your shots cleanly, and your opponent had a career day. Because she played great and won, and you played well and lost, does that mean you should walk off the court miserable? Of course not!

Stage 3 players play the ball, not the reputation on the other side of the net or the

> *Experience, which destroys innocence, also leads one back to it.*
>
> James Baldwin
> Author of Go Tell It On The Mountain

ghosts of past matches. They give 100 percent on the court and let the chips fall where they may.

Focus on your level of play, because you have control over that. If the score says you came in second, congratulate your opponent for being "too good" on that particular day.

Once you are able to do this, you'll find that you fall in love with the game all over again, this time for all the right reasons!

Chapter 19

Don't Call Me, I'll Call You

Every club has its share of tennis snobs. They strut around with their noses in the air, adorned in expensive outfits. They carry huge racket bags and an attitude that shouts, "Don't call me to play, I'll call you…if I deem you worthy."

We've all had our experiences with the dreaded tennis snob and it's never pleasant. From the moment you take the court you feel the avalanche of the snob's pressure and condescending attitude. You're immediately instructed where to play, how to play and to make sure that, above all, you "stay out of my way when I call for a shot."

The snob responds to your errors with body language that looks as if you've punched them in the stomach. They moan when you double fault, groan when you miss a volley and are particularly adept at convincing you that their errors are somehow your fault.

They'll complain about their partner after doubles losses and assure you that the only reason they're not at Wimbledon is that they had more important things to do with their life.

Snobbish behavior, on and off the tennis court, stems from insecurity, and one of the main reasons the tennis snob refuses to play with someone they feel is "below" them is that, deep down inside, they're insecure about their game and, quite often, themselves.

The tennis snob feeds on confrontation so the next time you find yourself across the net, or alongside, the dreaded snob, refuse to play his game. Though his words and actions may get your blood boiling, control your

"Is anyone here good enough to play with me?"

emotions and rise above it.   Here are three anti-snob strategies to get you through the match.

1.   Agree with the snob. When his words or body language scream out, "How could you miss that easy shot?" agree with him and say, "You're right, I should have had it." By agreeing, you'll immediately diffuse the situation.
2.   Ignore the snob. The snob can only get to you if you let him. Ignore his glare and move on to the next point.
3.   Laugh. The next time the snob makes you want to smack him over the head with your racket, smile and let out a small laugh. Steve Wilson, founder of the World Laughter Tour Inc., an organization that promotes therapeutic laughter, says that "under acute stress, the two hemispheres of the brain become disconnected. Laughter works as a relaxation response and calms the system. One of the myths is that laughter is trivial," he says. "It's very powerful."

The snob inside us all

Whether we're in a lesson situation, a practice match or social round robin, there is a general feeling that only by playing with people at or above our level will we improve or enjoy the game.

The fact is, there is something to be gained each and every time you step onto the tennis court, regardless of the level of the person across the net from you. When you step out onto the court there are three scenarios:

1.   The other player is stronger than you.
2.   The other player is at your level.
3.   The other player is weaker than you.

Here are a few tips to help you get the most out of your time on the court, regardless of who's on the other side of the net.

Hanging in there with better players

If you find yourself to be the weakest player on the court, your goal is to raise your game. You'll undoubtedly be nervous, particularly if one or, heaven forbid, more of the other players on the court are true tennis snobs.

To combat your nerves, keep your feet moving, focus solely on the ball and prepare your racket as quickly as possible. Pay attention to your breathing. When we get nervous we often have a tendency to hold our breath and this just increases the tension inside our bodies.

Just before you feel your racket contact the ball, make a concentrated effort to breathe out, or let out a strong grunt. It may sound funny but give it a shot. It does help to relieve stress and it certainly works for Maria Sharapova and Serena Williams.

When you're on the court with a better player don't take unnecessary risks and attempt shots you don't yet have. Chase down every shot and limit your unforced errors.

If your opponent hits at a faster pace then you're used to, fight the inevitable urge to try to keep up with their power. Prepare quicker, shorten your strokes and speed up your footwork.

I always like to compare playing against big hitters to lifting weights: If you're used to lifting ten pounds and then pick up twelve, it initially seems too heavy. After a while, though, you get used to the extra weight. The same is true on the tennis court. While your big hitting opponents at first seem too hot to handle, after a while you'll adjust to their pace.

If they like to attack the net, keep your groundstrokes deep or come in yourself. When they do take the net, aim low at their feet and hit lots of lobs. The overhead is an exhausting shot to execute and if you can make your opponent hit two or three each time they come to the net, you may very well wear them out.

If they're a human backboard, don't try to out steady them. Make your way to the net and force them to hit their groundstrokes under pressure. Or, you can try to bring them to the net, as most baseliners aren't particularly comfortable hitting volleys and overheads.

Keep them on the court for as long as possible. Take your time in between points and at the changeovers. The key is to focus on getting lots of balls back. Show them that you're not going to roll over just because they're "supposed" to be better than you. Make them prove it.

Playing an equal

When you play with someone at your level, your main challenge will be psychological. A match against two players of equal ability is usually one of patience decided by just a few points at key moments. Be the more patient player and minimize your unforced errors.

Work hard to keep your concentration intact by focusing intently on the ball. Get a high percentage of first serves in, be certain to return your opponent's serve and play your game.

If you are a baseliner, keep the ball deep, move your opponent around and refuse to miss. If you like to attack the net, wait for the right opportunity. Construct points and use your patterns instead of trying for low percentage big shots.

Since your level is equal to that of your opponent, prepare yourself for a long match and vow to be the more determined, focused and patient player.

Playing with someone weaker

When you take to the court with someone you feel is below your level, you've got to suppress the snob inside of you that's bursting to yell out, "This is going to be a waste of my time." It is not going to be a waste of your time—if you approach it with the proper attitude.

If you view the match as a waste of your precious time, it will be. However, if you see it as an opportunity to work on your game, you can get just as much out of the session as you would if you were playing with a stronger player.

Now is the time to work on that Continental grip your pro wants you to get used to at the net. Practice your new slice backhand and, when serving, hit only that topspin serve you're trying to get down.

If you're more comfortable at the baseline, force yourself to come to the net. If you're a serve and volley player, stay back and work on your groundstrokes. If your opponent hits a slower ball than you, practice taking their shots on the rise.

If they have a great forehand but a horrific backhand, hit every ball to their forehand. Yes, I know it's their stronger shot, but by hitting to their strength you'll not only be working on controlling your shots, you'll also be assured of getting a good ball back.

Pretend you're a pro

Have you ever noticed that during lessons with your pro, you're able to keep the ball going forever? Or, when playing practice points, he or she is able to make you move, stretch and struggle yet still allow you to return their shots?

This is because your pro has superb control. When you play with a weaker player, try to develop that level of control. Believe me, it is not easy to hit the ball exactly to your opponent's strike zone.

A quick aside: When I have my students practice hitting right to each other as a means of developing their control, there's always one member of the group who says, "If I hit right to them in practice, I'll hit right to them in a game." Well, with all due respect, that's a naive statement and only says that the player is not thinking when they're playing.

Tennis, in its simplest form, is hitting the ball to a target. When you practice, if that target is a player not only will you improve your control, you'll hit a lot of balls because your practice partner will be able to return them. If you develop the control to hit right to someone in practice, you'll have the control to hit it away from them during a match—just change your target.

Try to prolong the points so that you can hit more balls and work on your fitness and footwork. Chase down every ball and if your opponent hits a ball that lands an inch or two out, hit it back and keep the rally alive. The more balls you hit, the more practice you get.

Tennis legend Jimmy Connors was taught by his coach, Gloria, who also happened to be his mother, to chase after and hit back every ball in practice, whether it was in or out. She wanted Jimbo to get used to running after everything and to never let up. I think it's a super concept.

If you're playing in a doubles game below your level, again, work on the areas of your game that are not yet ready for prime time. For example, your serve and volley game, poaching, attacking a weak serve, finesse, lobbing your return of serve over the server's partner, etc. Remember, you're practicing, so don't worry about winning points.

By the way, if you have a partner who's much weaker than you, encourage them but, above all, don't coach them unless they ask.

Yes, everyone wants to play "up" but many forget that each time they play "up" the person they are playing with is playing down to play with them. It's a two way street. Don't be selfish and don't be a snob. Play with anyone and everyone.

Adopt a weaker player as your personal protégé. Invite them to play and try to help them improve though not in a condescending manner. Perhaps the most important thing you'll gain from hitting with a weaker player is the satisfaction of knowing that you've helped someone else with their tennis. Do you remember how great you felt the first time a stronger player asked you to hit with them? I do.

The tennis snob can attack us from the other side of the net or inside our own minds. By following these strategies, you'll be able to take the snob down in straight sets!

Chapter 20

Remaining Friends

We've all had that special pro that introduced us to tennis and made the game an important part of our lives. With you since your tennis infancy, in many ways your pro has served (no pun intended) as your tennis parent.

He was there when you chose your first racket. He taught you the strokes and strategy. He showed you how to change your over-grip and was nearby when you played your first "real" match. He's suffered with you during your crushing losses and celebrated with you when you finally defeated your long-time nemesis. Not only has he been your tennis teacher, he's become a good friend, which makes it all the more difficult when the time comes to move on to another instructor.

Relationships grow stale and seeing the same face week after week and being taught in the same style over a long period of time can get tedious. If you advance to the national level of competition or above, you may feel as if you want a coach "who's been there." No one is at fault. It just becomes time to move on.

A new pro can bring a fresh eye and new perspective to your game. All teaching professionals have particular methods of looking at a student and areas of the game they feel are most important.

I personally feel that good footwork is the most important element of tennis, while other pros feel that the strokes are the most vital elements of the game. When these pros see a student, they look first at their stroking patterns. When I see them, I first check out their feet, because I feel that their footwork dictates their stroking

pattern. One approach is not better than the other—
they're just different.

The itch to switch

The most common reason players cite for wanting a new
pro is that they feel as if they're not improving quickly
enough. If you're frustrated with your lack of progress, sit
down and discuss it with your pro. There's a good chance
he's feeling the same.

Tell him your concerns and explain what you're
looking for from your lessons. Let him know what he does
that you like and dislike, as well as things you wish he
would do. Be honest with him and give him a chance to
make adjustments. A true professional can and will. Also,
be sure to listen to his comments with an open mind. You
should both learn from each other.

A successful student/teacher relationship consists
of the two of you working toward a common goal: your
improvement and long-term enjoyment of the game. The
pro's job is to provide you with his expertise and make
your time together enjoyable. Your job is to practice and
apply that expertise.

If you simply take your lesson once a week and
don't step on a court in between, you can't realistically
expect to make a great leap in your level of play. If you're
not practicing the techniques your pro has shown you
with the understanding that change and improvement
take time, you're not really giving his methods a fair shot.

Also, keep in mind that moving to the higher levels
of the game can be a long and bumpy process. Players
who want a quick fix often jump from one pro to the next
in search of "the secret" that will take them to the top.
Beware of pros that promise a "magic method." There are
no shortcuts to becoming a high-level tennis player.

Geoff Norton says, "pro hopping can be a bigger hindrance than assistance. Moving from one instructor to another usually does little more than confuse the player. In many cases, he has so many thoughts bouncing around in his head that his game actually gets worse."

When a change is inevitable

Once you've made your decision to switch pros, the key to a successful transition is communication. I've seen players who can't bear to speak to the pro face to face cancel their five-year standing lesson by simply leaving a message at the club.

Not only is this extremely rude but you'll both feel awkward when you run into each other at the club, which you will. And when he sees you taking a lesson with one of his colleagues, it may cause tension between the two pros.

Pick up the phone and speak to the pro directly or, better yet, sit down with him and honestly explain your reasons for leaving. Simply tell him that you want another instructor to take a look at your game and offer his thoughts on what you can do to improve.

It doesn't have to be a nasty, uncomfortable confrontation. The best pros will understand how difficult it is for you to initiate this conversation and do everything they can to ease your stress.

Tom Veneziano, author of the popular Tennis Warrior series (More info: tenniswarrior.com), says, "if the pro is doing a good job, he should not take this personally. If he's been doing a poor job, maybe he should take it personally and learn from it!"

Thank the pro for all he has done for you and your game and leave the door open for future lessons. Though the grass may seem greener elsewhere, you may well find that your current pro is the best one for you. Be sure not to burn that bridge.

Keep in mind that a true professional will understand your feelings and not be offended by your desire to take lessons with someone else. Many pros will even suggest that their students try someone new if they feel they've hit a roadblock. They'll also make an effort to speak with your new instructor and tell him or her about you, your game, and style of learning.

A teaching professional's concern should be for your continued improvement and enjoyment of the game. There is not a pro on the face of the planet that has not had a student leave them for another instructor. It's part of the business. By communicating openly there should be no hard feelings. The pro will appreciate your honesty and the friendship you've developed over the years will remain intact.

Chapter 21

Commandments Of Social Tennis

It's match point. You're about to hit your second serve on the verge of your biggest win of the season. You toss the ball and, just as you're about to make contact, a cell phone rings on the next court. You flinch and your second serve hits your partner on the back of the neck. You've double faulted, your partner's in agony and you're fuming!

You look toward the next court and see one of the players talking into her cell phone, discussing where she's going for lunch. The three other players on her court are clearly furious as well as she rudely keeps them waiting.

Cell phones are just one breach of tennis etiquette that have infected the social tennis scene over the past few years. After talking to hundreds of players around the world, I've come up with my 10 Commandments of Social Tennis.

Follow these tips and you'll never again have trouble finding people to play with—they'll find you.

1. Be Punctual
- Time is always an issue on the social scene so keep these issues in mind.
- Be on time. You risk alienating your partners, besides wasting valuable and often expensive court time, if you don't arrive on time. Set your watch 10 minutes ahead if you are habitually late. Also, if you know in advance that you can't stay for the entire time, don't agree to the game.

- Wait your turn. I know you're eager to play, but if your court is being used, wait patiently until your time starts. Let those occupying your court see that you're there but do not enter the court early or in the middle of a point.
- Finish on time. When your time is up, get off the court. It is not appropriate to ask if you can finish the game or play one more point.

2. Bring the balls

- Always keep a new can of balls in your bag in case no one else on your court brings them. I know Fred hasn't bought a can of balls since the turn of the century but it's too small a battle to fight. Keep the peace and provide the balls. By the way, those balls that were only used once will not do.

3. Don't Try to Win the Warm-up

- Even in a competitive situation in which you're trying to get a feel for your opponent's game, it's still common courtesy to help them warm-up their shots. Don't go for winners and allow your opponent to warm up all of their shots.

4. Retrieve and return balls courteously

- When your ball ends up on the next court, wait until the point is over, and then politely ask for your ball. It's also considered good etiquette to apologize for interrupting the game. Be sure to thank the players when they return your ball.
- When a ball from the next court rolls across yours on a crucial point, resist the urge to roll your eyes and let out a groan. Even if it was at break point, the players on the other court

didn't mean to hit it onto your court. Graciously return it to them and play a let.

5. Accept your mistakes

- No matter how badly you may be playing or losing, keep a positive attitude and your excuses to yourself. No one's interested, and you'll only sound foolish.

6. Treat your opponent with respect

- You're not at war. You're out there together to get a good workout and have some fun. Compliment their good shots, and at the end of the match shake hands and say, "Well played"— win or lose.

7. When in doubt, call the ball in

- My guess is that you're not playing at Wimbledon, and if you are there will be people to call the lines for you. In a social game or league match, if you can't tell if the ball was inside or outside of the line, give your opponent the benefit of the doubt and call the ball good. There are few things in life worth fighting over. A tennis match is not one of them.

8. Be a positive partner

- You're his partner, not his coach. Offer support, not instruction.

9. Clean up the court

- Be sure to remove all balls, cans, water bottles, towels and anything else you brought to the court. If you're playing on a clay court, it's also a classy move to sweep it if the equipment is available.

And last, but not least. . .

10.   Shut off your cell phone.

- The President is not calling to ask for your advice and Maria Sharapova is not calling you for a game. Leave the number of the club with your friends and family. If there is an emergency, you can be reached via the front desk.

- If you are playing at a facility with no receptionist, leave your cell phone on, but put the ring function on the silent mode. Check it at every changeover if you must. There are exceptions, such as doctors on call, so be tolerant.

Tennis was conceived as a sport of finesse and etiquette, to be played by ladies and gentlemen. Follow these 10 Commandments of Social Tennis and you'll be a popular player wherever you go!

You can discover more about a person in an hour of play than in a year of discussion.

Plato

"We really need to get together for lunch sometime."

Chapter 22

Play Your Best Forever

Though we may try to deny it, at some point we'll all begin to feel the effects of aging. Our clothes become tighter, but we're much more willing to go along with the discomfort than we are to admit that our bodies are perhaps spreading out a bit. We're stiffer after a tough match, but we rationalize that by saying that we really did a lot of running.

Eventually, we can no longer ignore the obvious and are forced to admit that we're not kids anymore. The same effort simply does not produce the same results and we come to truly understand the phrase, "the mind is willing, but the body is not."

For some players, this inevitability is too much to

> *We are not limited by our old age; we are liberated by it.*
>
> Stu Mittleman
> World-class ultra-marathoner

bear and, as soon as their performance on the court begins to decline, they get frustrated and say, "What's the point? If I can't play as well as I used to, why play at all? It's time to try golf."

Bite your tongue! Middle age and the years that follow should be the most enjoyable time of your tennis life. By the time you hit your late 40s or 50s, the kids have probably flown the nest and you're relatively secure in your career. Now it's your time!

Experts at the American Anti-Aging Society say that as science progresses, those of you reading this book can possibly live to be 120-130 years old! That's a lot of years to enjoy roaming the courts. To do so, you need to come up with a strategy to take father time deep into the third set.

Getting older doesn't mean you have to get old

There is no genetic predisposition that says we have to get fat and stiff as we get older. Dr. Kenneth Cooper, the "inventor" of aerobics and founder of the Cooper Wellness Program in Dallas, TX (More info: cooperinst.org), states that, "what we previously attributed to the physical effects of aging are, in reality, adaptive responses.

These things occur in our bodies not so much because we grow older, but because we become more sedentary as we grow older." The decline, says Dr. Cooper, is therefore largely "a matter of rusting out, not wearing out."

The rusting process is a gradual one. We eat and drink more, exercise less and, before we know it, the aches and pains start creeping in. Our bodies hurt, which only gives us an excuse to be even less active and to eat and drink more. The needle on the scale creeps upward, and before we know it, we become hostages inside our own bodies.

Certainly, as we get older, our bodies will change and while we can't completely stop the aging process, we can greatly minimize its effects with a few simple strategies.

Proper nutrition becomes even more important

Chocolate donuts and soda for breakfast, three fast food hamburgers, large fries, washed down with another soda for lunch. That was my nutritional program for much of my twenties and I loved it! Thanks to a lot of hours on the tennis court and a cast iron stomach I didn't gain 50 pounds or make myself sick.

Though both those meals still sound good to me, I've learned that I can no longer enjoy them every day. As an older player, your body needs efficient fuel so that you can play your best and also recover for the next day's match.

Here's a sample diet that will get your ready for, take you through and help you recover from your next big match.

Pre-game meal (one hour prior to taking the court): Wheat pasta with a slice of whole wheat toast. A cup of strawberries and two glasses of water. Absolutely no carbonation with your meal.

During the match: Water, water, water. Every fifteen minutes and at every changeover. Stay away from eating during the match. You don't want your body working to digest food while you're playing.

After the match: It's all about recovery so go with protein such as skinless chicken, fish, or even a small piece of lean red meat. Drink more water and even treat yourself to a glass of wine. The wine will open up your capillaries, which will help your blood flow through your body. This blood flow will promote the healing of the many small tears and strains your muscles suffered during the match.

Dr. Andrew Weil, (More info: drweil.com.) author of the book Healthy Aging offers the following general dietary guidelines to not only "promote optimum health" but also to "reduce the risk of age-related diseases"
* Aim for variety.
* Include as much fresh food as possible.

- Minimize your consumption of processed foods and fast food.
- Eat an abundance of fruits and vegetables.

Water, water, water

As always, be sure to drink plenty of water, whether you're on the court or off.. The water we drink helps our bodies digest and absorb vitamins and nutrients. It also detoxifies our liver and kidneys and helps our digestion. By the way, drinking water has also shown to help with weight loss.

If we become dehydrated, our blood literally thickens and our body then has to work harder to circulate it throughout our body. As a result, we find it harder to concentrate, feel fatigued, and just simply "run out of gas."

Begin each day with a big glass of water. It'll wake up your body and give you an early energy boost. Carry a water bottle and sip from it throughout the day. Take your body weight and divide it by two. That's how many ounces of water you should drink each day.

By the way, you don't need to spend a fortune buying "fashionable" bottled water. In most cases, tap water is fine. Be sure to stop drinking water two hours before bedtime, otherwise you'll feel as if you're sprinting from the baseline to the net throughout the night as you repeatedly get up to go to the bathroom.

> *We are all going to die, rich or poor, and I prefer to die in good health.*
>
> Beppe Merio
> World-class player of the 1950s

Keep an eye on your weight

The average person gains approximately 1 pound each year after the age of 25, which means by the time we're 55, we've gained 30 pounds! In addition to slowing us down around the court, this excess weight forces our bodies to work harder to function and our muscles and joints have to support that weight.

If you're a 4.0 level player and above, your tennis matches should provide you with a great workout that will help you to maintain a healthy weight as well as keep your heart strong.

If you're new to the game or have not yet reached a more advanced level, tennis alone probably will not be enough to keep your heart fit and your weight under control. To supplement your time on the court, take a Cardio Tennis class or spend some time walking on a treadmill or swimming laps in the pool. Your heart and your waistline will thank you! You'll also see a definite improvement in your game.

Eating slowly is also a great way to monitor your weight. It takes approximately five minutes for your brain to realize that your stomach is full. During those five minutes you can throw down a lot of unneeded calories. Eat slowly, enjoy your food, and learn to recognize when you're no longer hungry.

Magic fingers

A regular session with a massage therapist can go a long way toward working out the aches and strains that comes with years of pounding the courts. As we get older our bodies' capacity to bring oxygen to our muscles decreases. Massage promotes blood flow, which, in turn, brings oxygen to our muscles and allows them to function more effectively.

Deep tissue massage is recommended for tennis players because it not only helps with the maintenance of our bones, muscles and tissues, it also promotes the healing of minor strains and sprains.

Pete Sampras used to travel with his own masseuse and received daily massages after workouts and matches. If you don't have Sampras' budget, reward yourself once or twice a month. You'll feel twenty years younger.

Sleep hygiene

In Time magazine, Robert Stickgold, a cognitive neuroscientist at Harvard Medical School said that "many of us live on the edge of sleep starvation." Sleep can be just as important to our minds and bodies as the food we eat, yet 71 percent of American adults do not get the recommended eight hours of sleep a night.

As tennis players, sleep deprivation can affect our energy on the court both physically and emotionally. Sleep also helps us recover from the stresses of play. This becomes particularly important as we get older. If you're having trouble sleeping, try the following:

- Stay away from naps. Naps can throw off your body's internal clock and make it more difficult for you to sleep at night.
- Avoid caffeine, alcohol and nicotine. All three can disrupt your sleep patterns.
- Keep your bedroom dark and cool. As soon as you wake-up, expose yourself to either a bright light or the sun. This will help your body regulate its biological clock.
- Play your tennis in the morning and afternoon. Your body may find it difficult to come down from

the excitement of your game, so play your tennis earlier in the day.

- Stay away from heavy meals and fluids before bedtime. Both can interfere with your sleep.
- Have some turkey before you go to bed. Turkey contains an amino acid called tryptophan that helps your brain produce the chemical serotonin, which helps your body relax. Tryptophan can also be found in milk and peanuts. So have a small glass of warm milk and a half a turkey sandwich for a good night's sleep.

Adjust your equipment

If you begin to notice that your eyes aren't as sharp as they once were, try switching to an oversized racket with a bigger sweet spot. Also, an extra-long frame will make some of those harder to reach shots more reachable.

Two experts in the area of racket technology offer some additional helpful hints. David Bone, the Executive Director of the U.S. Racquet Stringers Association (More info: usrsa.com) suggests that "if you find that your shots aren't as powerful or as deep as they once were, try stringing your racket a few pounds looser."

James Martin, the Editor-in-Chief at Tennis magazine (More info: Tennis.com) says that "another key factor as you get older is using racquets that are easier on the arm. Most of the major companies have specifically designed rackets to create a softer feel."

Regardless of what type of racket you use, be sure to keep your strings and grips fresh as both will provide cushioning for your arm, wrist and shoulder. A general rule of thumb says that you should get your racket restrung as many times per year as you play each week. Your grips should be changed at least that often.

Finally, make sure to use new, lively balls every time you step onto the court. Balls become heavier the more they're hit and, as a result, become more stressful to your arm, wrist and shoulder. Finish your match and then give the balls to the pro for his lessons.

Take a break

Rest and recuperation are just as important as nutrition and exercise. After a few hard sets of tennis or vigorous exercise, the body is worn down physically and mentally. Listen to your body and become acquainted with its signals. For me, my knees and lower back start creaking and I begin to play and behave impatiently when I do too much.

In my youth, I could push past those clues and still be OK. Now that I'm in my late 40s, I can't get away with that, so I take two days off to avoid injury. If your body feels tired, it is. Pain is your body's signal that something is wrong. Give yourself time to recoup and recover. And if the pain or fatigue doesn't go away within a week to ten days, see your doctor.

When the body breaks down

The only sure-fire way to never suffer an athletic injury is to lead a sedentary life, but what fun is that? If you're active, odds are at some time you're going to suffer an injury. When that inevitability occurs, your number one concern becomes minimizing its effects.

Most tennis-related injuries can be treated by RICE, which stands for rest, ice, compression and elevation. By adhering to this formula, you will reduce the swelling that occurs when blood flows to an injured area.

If you can minimize the swelling immediately after the injury, you'll have much less pain and recover faster. Studies have shown that a mildly sprained ankle will heal in about half the time if you use RICE as opposed to doing nothing.

Sports medicine orthopedist, Dr. Andrew Bazos, who has treated professional athletes and weekend warriors alike for over a decade says that "identifying the type of injury early is key to deciding whether it's safe to play through the pain or if rest or more aggressive treatment is indicated." Bazos, Medical Director of New York's Madison Square Garden, offers a few suggestions for prevention and treatment of three of tennis's most common injuries.

Tennis elbow

Tennis elbow is an inflammation of the tendons attaching the forearm muscles to the elbow. It's generally caused by either playing too much tennis or hitting the ball incorrectly.

Using a grip that is too big or too small, dead balls or dead strings or too heavy a racket can also contribute to the inflammation. The stress builds over time, irritating or tearing the tendon. When you experience those initial twinges, get ice on it right away.

Most tennis clubs have ice available for any emergency situation but you should also keep a ready supply in your refrigerator at home. Take a half dozen paper cups, fill them with water and put them in your freezer. Once they're frozen, peel off an inch of the paper cup around the top and use this "popsicle" to massage the painful area with ice. Massage your elbow for about 15-20 minutes.

Once the pain subsides, strengthen you wrist and forearm by doing wrist curls and reverse wrist curls. Simply squeezing a soft, rubber ball also helps. Treating elbow pain as soon as it appears can spare you years of agony and more extensive medical treatments.

The moment you feel that first twinge your elbow, head straight for your pro. Let him take a look at your strokes and see if you're doing something technique-wise that might be causing your pain

Pulled calf muscles

Because of the stop-and-start explosive movements of tennis, the calf plays an important role in every move you make. Unfortunately, as we get older, our muscles and tendons begin to lose their elasticity. The result, for many tennis players, is lower leg pulls.

If you feel pain in your calf, take a few days off. Apply the RICE formula and once it begins to feel better, slowly stretch it out. Wall push-ups are a great way to stretch the calf. Simply put one foot as far away from a wall as you can and keep that heel on the ground. Your other leg remains a few inches from the wall.

With bent elbows, lean into the wall, keeping your rear heel on the ground. Hold the stretch for 15-20 seconds and then push yourself back up. Repeat two or three times before switching legs.

To prevent calf muscle pulls, strengthen your calf muscles as well as stretch them. A great strengthening exercise is the Toe Raise. Stand on the edge of a stair with your heels over the edge. Rise up on your toes, count to 10 and then lower your heels below the stair as far as you can to stretch the tendon.

Do 10 repetitions or until you begin to feel some fatigue in your calves. As you get stronger, you can do one leg at a time or hold a light weight to increase resistance.

Knee injuries

Your knees take a heavy pounding as they help you move about the court, particularly if you play on hard courts. Treat the basic soreness with RICE, but if the pain doesn't go away in a few days, see your doctor. You may have to have X-rays or an MRI (magnetic resonance imaging) to check for torn cartilage or ligaments.

To help prevent knee injuries, keep the muscles, tendons and ligaments that surround your knees strong. Leg extensions and leg curls on a weight bench or universal-style machine are excellent exercises. If you don't have access to exercise equipment buy some ankle weights and do these exercise while sitting in a chair.

Most tennis-related injuries are minor and can be treated with basic common sense. However, if your pain doesn't go away after a week to ten days, if it comes on suddenly or is severe, see your doctor. An ounce of prevention is worth a pound of cure.

A healthy mind

Have you ever noticed that some people become much more serious, judgmental and cynical as they get older? Minor things become major issues, and many people seem to forget how to laugh. Depression is a major concern among senior citizens as they come to terms with their own mortality and that of their friends. Many lose their motivation, retire to the couch and begin the rusting process.

The keys to maintaining a healthy mind are stimulation and laughter. Tennis provides both. Many senior players tell me

> *I'm growing older but not up.*
>
> Jimmy Buffett
> Singer

that their involvement in the game has given them a reason to get up in the morning and something to look forward to every day.

Become actively involved with the sport. All tennis associations are looking for volunteers to help with their programs, events and tournaments. Write a tennis column for the town newspaper or apply for a part time job at the front desk or in the pro shop of your local tennis club. Maybe you could coach a high school team or get involved with a program teaching disadvantaged children. Being around kids is a great way to stay young.

The choice is yours

Society tells us that as we get older we should slow down and act our age. We're told to stop playing, on and off the court. That's ridiculous! It's when we stop playing that we do get old!

Denmark's Harry Meistrup played tennis three times a week at the youthful age of 103, and Dodo Cheney, 89, is still adding to her record of over 300 National titles. There's no reason why you shouldn't continue to play, and enjoy, tennis as you move into your 70s, 80s and 90s.

> *You don't get to choose how or when you die. You only get to choose how you're going to live.*
>
> Joan Baez
> Singer

The game of tennis always becomes more exciting in the third set. So should the game of life. Middle age and beyond is your time. Get out there, be active and have the time of your life.

TREASURE THOSE MAGIC MOMENTS

I was getting ready to call it a day when three of my club's members ambled over to the courts. They explained that their fourth couldn't make it and wondered if I'd fill in.

I grabbed my racket, met the three men on court 1 and sixty minutes later walked off the court having enjoyed what will forever be one of my most special experiences on a tennis court.

It wasn't the level of play that made the game so special, nor was it the excitement of the match because I have no idea who won. What made this game so special was the cast of characters I was on the court with.

On the opposite side of the net there was 84-year-old Bill and 87-year-old Bob. My partner was "the kid," 79-year-old Ben. That's 250 years combined and, if you throw in my 42 years, the grand total of all the players on court #1 that Sunday was 292 years.

I was partnered with "the kid," Ben, for two reasons: He had just taken up the game a year ago and had recently had knee and hip replacement surgery. The others figured that, that at my youthful age of 42, I could make up for his lack of experience and mobility.

As the match began, all three men assumed their "ready position," which, in their 80s, didn't look a whole lot different than their general posture. Bill and Bob both stared me down, though I was not certain that they could see that I was preparing to serve. Just to be sure, I yelled out as I tossed the ball, "Okay, here we go!"

The points were long, strategic and usually decided by a winning drop shot or lob. There was no power for two reasons.

First, most players in their 70s and 80s cannot generate much power and, more important, players of that generation learned a different type of game than we see today.

Bill, Bob and Ben are from an era in which matches were decided by the more strategic player., Not the one who could hit the ball the hardest. Our match more resembled a game of chess and was a test of finesse and creativity.

In between points, during extended change-over periods and at least one bathroom break for each player (myself included), good natured trash-talking was at a premium. Both Bob and Bill told Ben that his "new parts needed oil," Ben teased Bob about his "hot date" the night before with 79-year-old Pat, and all three told me that fifty years ago they would have wiped up the court with me.

I cannot remember a time where I had more fun on a tennis court than I did that day with my three super seniors. The fact that, at their ages, they were still playing and enjoying tennis was fantastic, but it was more the camaraderie that the three shared, and allowed me to share, that made the match so memorable.

These seniors, and countless others around the world, play tennis for the sheer love of the game. Who wins and loses is irrelevant. These players are so far removed from their egos on the court that they are able to laugh at their mistakes and just enjoy being there.

Bill and Bob had played for many, many years, certainly at a better level than they play at today, but it didn't matter to them. There was no sadness in the realization that they used to be able to hit a particular shot or reach a certain ball.

Quite the contrary, they were more than happy, even grateful, that they were still able to get out there and hit the ball around a bit.

Then there's Ben, who was new to the game and like a kid in a toy store. He has his new racket, high-tech shoes, his state-of-the-art knee brace, and is training for, and counting the days until, he is eligible for the 80 and over tournaments.

I think we finished two sets, but amidst the talking and laughing, we all lost track of the score and claimed victory. We sat down for a beer, traded war stories, did a bit more trash talking and then walked out to the parking lot and waited for Bob's wife to pick him up. Bill informed me that "Bob doesn't drive any more because he doesn't see so well, as you probably noticed by his line calls."

While we waited, I learned that the reason their fourth, John, couldn't make it was because, at age 91, he had just passed away. It was John's father who had started this group 60 years ago with Bill and Bob's fathers and another gentleman whose name escaped them.

Through the years, Bill, Bob and John would fill in when needed and eventually, as each original member passed away, his son would take his place. John had been playing with another fellow named Jerry and when Jerry died, John was the one who literally got Ben out of his rocking chair and onto the tennis court. "We needed a and fourth," Bob said, "so John convinced Ben to get off his fat butt and take up the game." "Best thing that ever happened to me," said Ben.

"Now we have to find someone else," Bill said sadly. As Bob's wife pulled up to the club, I found myself asking if I could join them. They all smiled at each other, Bob said, "If you think you're up to it kid."

Chapter 23

Being The Best
Tennis Parent Ever

Tennis truly is the sport for a lifetime and what better gift can a parent give to their children than an activity that they'll be able to enjoy throughout their entire lives?

While improving our skills and winning matches feel great, they pale in comparison to being on the court with one of your children. Introducing your kids to tennis in the proper manner will go a long way toward insuring that they enjoy a long life in the game.

When is the right time to start?

Every child develops concentration and coordination at their own pace but usually between the ages of four and seven is a good time to introduce them to the game. Take your little one to the courts when you play and let him see how much you enjoy tennis.

Bring him onto the court and play catch with him, or let him practice hitting a balloon up in the air with his hand. This will help develop his hand-eye coordination, and he'll get a thrill out of being on a tennis court "just like mom and dad." Strokes and technique can wait, just let him have fun. If he associates stepping onto a tennis court with fun and games, he'll eventually want to play.

Once you feel he's ready for formal instruction, you'll have to decide if you want to go with group or private lessons. I suggest group lessons with a friend or two. They're less expensive and he'll feel more comfortable trying something new if he's with a few friends. Group lessons are also a great way for your child to begin to develop their social skills. In addition, some children are inhibited by having the spotlight on them, and a group lesson avoids the pressure of one-on-one instruction.

Choosing a pro

Ask your friends who they or their children take lessons from and then take a ride over to the club and watch the pro give a lesson.

A beginning child needs a pro who is enthusiastic, energetic and who likes kids. Teaching young children can be extremely challenging,

The mediocre teacher tells; the good teacher explains; the superior teacher demonstrates, and the great teacher inspires.

William Arthur Ward

on many levels, so the pro must be patient and able to express himself clearly. People learn in different ways so he must be able to distinguish your child's learning style and adjust his teaching accordingly.

The most important thing to look for is the expressions on the students' faces. Are they smiling and having fun or do they seem bored? By watching the prospective pro interact with his young students you'll get a feel for if he would work well with your child.

DON'T BE FOOLED BY THE TROPHIES

I always get a kick out of listening to people talk about their tennis instructors because they inevitably gloat about what a great player they are or were:

"Bob played # 1 for Florida State in 1977."

...Like father like son

"Sam is ranked # 3 in New England in his age division."

"Betty had a win over someone who had a win over a player who went three sets with Chris Evert when Chrissie was 12."

While those are certainly all impressive accomplishments, the fact that Bob, Sam or Betty have a closet full of trophies, a boatload of newspaper clippings, or a serve that breaks the sound barrier has virtually nothing to do with whether that person is qualified to teach the game

While a teaching pro certainly needs to have the technical skills to demonstrate the game's various techniques, feed the ball at different cadences and speeds, and hit at a level that can push his or her students, there are many other, much more important ingredients that go into the recipe that makes a superb teaching professional. Here are a few:

Knowledge: A good teaching professional should know the advantages and disadvantages of the Eastern, Continental, Semi-Western and Western grips as they relate to every shot in the game. They should be able to offer you different stroking options, explain the various footwork patterns and advise you on the latest rackets, shoes, strings and grips.

Communication skills: Knowledge is key but equally important is the teaching professional's ability to convey that knowledge to his or her students in an easy to understand, entertaining manner. People learn in different ways and a good teaching pro is able to figure out whether a student responds best to visual demonstrations or auditory instructions. This is not a skill that is learned at 5-5 in the third set. It is learned through training and spending hundreds of hours on the court with all different types of people.

Flexibility: There is no one tried and proven way to teach the game. Many great players will try to clone themselves through their students. The true professional has an approach to the game that he or she feels is the best and is able, and willing, to adjust that method to fit the student's needs and ability.

Patience: There is nothing more challenging than watching one of your students swing and miss, or miss-hit, ball after ball for sixty minutes. Think of fingernails being scraped down a backboard and you have the effect that a teaching pro experiences when a student hits one ball after another off the side of their frame.

Though a struggling student can be frustrating for the instructor, the feeling is much worse for the student. The experienced pro knows this and is able, through encouraging and often joking comments, to not only keep the student's spirits up but to also help them work through their difficulty. They remember how difficult it was for them to learn the game and tell the student stories about how they struggled with the same shot when they first started.

Many great players lack this character trait as it relates to tennis. They've been playing the game for such a long time that hitting the ball has become as natural to them as blinking their eyes. It's often quite difficult for them to understand how someone can't hit the ball in the middle of the strings or execute a slice serve. It's said that patience is a virtue. For the tennis teaching professional it is as much a necessity as a racket and basket of balls.

Enthusiasm: As in any business, the good pros are there for more than the paycheck. They love what they do and you can feel it from the moment you walk on the court. They greet you with an eagerness and enthusiasm that's infectious.

It should be all about the student. The pro is there for you and everything that he or she says and does must come from that perspective.

Yes, if you are an elite player, it does help to have, a pro who's "been there." Brad Gilbert is an excellent example of this. He's played Wimbledon, the U.S. Open etc. so he understands what it takes to win at that level. He also has an incredible understanding of the game's strategies and the ability to point out a player's strengths, weaknesses, and patterns. Would I trust him to teach a complete beginner, with limited athletic ability, who's not sure if they really want to play tennis? Not necessarily.

When you're looking for someone to teach you or your children, don't be blinded by the light shining off a person's trophies. Do your research and make certain that the person you are considering has the knowledge, the communication and emotional skills and, most important, the desire to help your child become passionate about the game.

The proper equipment

Check with the club to see if they have any type of dress code but at most public facilities any athletic shorts and t-shirt will do, as will virtually any type of athletic sneakers. Stay away from running shoes because they lack the proper support for tennis.

The only initial investment you'll have to make is to buy your child a racket and, no, Mom or Dad's old racket will not do. You don't want your son or daughter to try swinging a racket that's too big, too long or too heavy for him or her. It will only make the game seem much more difficult and a lot less fun.

The key consideration when buying a racket for your child is the racket's length. This is usually determined using their height as a reference. Here are some general guidelines to follow:

Table 23-1

Child's Height	Racket Length
3'10" and below	21"
3'11-4'5"	23"
4'6"-4'11"	25" or 26"
5' or taller	27" or longer

Speak to your pro or go to a tennis specialty shop where they can help you choose a racket with the correct grip and head size, length and weight for your child.

The big day

As you drive your child to his first tennis lesson, you'll undoubtedly be excited and, in the back of your mind, you'll be wondering if your child just might be the next Roger Federer or Lindsay Davenport.

Push those thoughts aside and remember that tennis is simply something new that he's going to try. Express this to your son or daughter and tell them that if they like it, great! If not, no big deal. This will help ease any pressure they may be feeling, as well as open their mind to the new experience.

When you get to the courts, introduce her to the pro and then go away. Let the pro do his job and don't interfere. Do not sit on the side of the court, and, above all, don't talk to your child during his lesson.

It's his time to be alone with his teacher. Bring a book, sit up in the lobby or a respectable distance from the court and read. Let her see that you're still there, but out of the way.

If your child is very young or sensitive, she may insist that you come to the court with her. That's fine but gradually wean yourself away.

After the lesson

Speak with the pro to find out what he's worked on, and ask for suggestions, drills and games that you can play with your child. Practice sessions, if handled properly, can be a real source of enjoyment for you and your new tennis player.

Practice at a time that suits both of you, and try to make it a regular activity, something that you both look forward to. Go over what the instructor taught him but don't preach or push your child to perform. Remember, practice sessions should be something that the child wants to do, rather than is required to do, so make them fun and stop when he wants to stop.

Support and reinforce the techniques that the pro has introduced during the lesson. If you have a question or disagreement regarding something the pro has told your child, do not contradict him in front of your child. Speak with the instructor privately.

Even though you may have won your last five league matches, the pro is the expert, and in most cases you should go along with the program he or she has devised.

Don't push them!

When our children were born, Kelley and I couldn't wait to get them started playing tennis. Confident that we'd "seen it all," we were certain we'd be able to introduce the game in a healthy, enjoyable manner. We had no interest in raising champions. We just wanted to give Mike, and later Katie, a chance to enjoy tennis throughout their lives.

We took them to the courts and then a funny thing happened—they both told us they didn't like tennis. We told them that we would never force them to do an activity they didn't like but urged them to give it another try. They did, but comments like "tennis is stupid" and "I hate tennis" starting popping out of their mouths.

We ran through the gamut of reasons why they didn't want to play. Perhaps, they didn't feel they could live up to people's expectations, or they resented tennis because it took Mom and Dad away from them each day. Maybe by not playing tennis, they felt they were establishing their independence—"Mom and Dad want us to, so we won't." Or maybe they just didn't like tennis.

Whatever the reasons, we were faced with a difficult decision: Should we allow our children to pass up what would undoubtedly be a tremendous opportunity to learn and enjoy a game they could play for the rest of their live, or should we force them to play tennis?

There really was no decision to make. We knew that forcing Mike and Katie to play tennis would only turn them off to the sport forever and, far more important, damage our relationship with them. If, after a lesson or two, your child says he doesn't want to play anymore, don't push it. Back off and try again later.

As parents, there are enough areas where we are forced to put our feet down and insist. How our children conduct themselves, how they treat others, the necessity of honest effort in whatever they do, even wearing seat belts are far more important issues than whether or not they ever pick up a tennis racket. Kelley and I felt that to make tennis an issue would only create an unnecessary power struggle. We didn't want to win the battle and lose the war. So we backed off.

We must remember that our job as parents is to raise healthy, happy and productive individuals. Along the way, many battles will arise and we must decide which are worth fighting. Otherwise our kids will tune us out completely and miss the truly important messages we want to convey to them.

Though we didn't force our kids to play tennis we did insist that they do something physical—something of their choosing. The importance of health and exercise was one of those "important" messages that we wanted to get across to our children.

Do we feel funny every time one of our students says, "Your kids must be great tennis players"? Yes we do, a little bit. Do we feel a touch envious when we see some of our students hitting with their parents? At times.

Do we feel we made the right decision? Absolutely! Our kids know that we'd like for them to play tennis, and, in fact, they tease us about it. However, I truly believe that our decision strengthened our relationship and made them much more receptive to the other messages we wanted to get across. Our success as parents is not measured by the number of trophies our kids bring home, but rather by the type of people they become.

If your kids initially resist tennis, don't push it. Back off and offer it to them at a later date. You never know when the interest might arise. My son, Mike, who's now 19, has developed an interest in tennis. We play when we can but the decision to play is always his—as it should be.

The bigger picture

Keep in mind that you are not trying to develop the next Andre Agassi or Venus Williams but rather let them experience the game and all it can offer.

Tennis can teach your child many lessons that will stay with them throughout their lives: commitment, discipline, sportsmanship, performance under pressure and teamwork.

The game should be fun and a release from the pressures kids face every day, both academically and socially. Teach your kids to compete within themselves and to try to be the best they can be. This will carry over into other, truly significant areas of their lives.

The care and feeding of a competitive junior

If your child does develop a passion for the game and moves on to competitive tennis, your role as a parent becomes even more complicated and critical!

Have you ever been to a junior tennis tournament? It can be quite a spectacle. You'll see parents jump out of their seats shouting instructions as their child prepares to serve. Or they'll shriek after she misses an easy volley. These are the same parents who applaud opponents' errors and sit on the side of the court during their child's lessons "helping the pro."

In the most frightening case of tennis parenting, one father placed drugs in his children's opponents' water bottles in an attempt to help them win. When one of those opponents fell asleep at the wheel while driving home after the match, crashed, and died, that parent was subsequently arrested, convicted, and sentenced to eight years in prison.

Others operate on a much more subtle level. They use facial expressions, body language or quiet actions to convey their displeasure. To the casual observer, they appear harmless, and their judgmental attitude often goes undetected, except by the ones whom they impact the most—their children.

In the high-pressure atmosphere that "tennis parents" can create, kids often feel that they're playing for their parents' attention and affection. They feel as if they are constantly being judged and evaluated. It's devastating for a child to look up at the one person in the world who is supposed to provide unconditional love and support and see anger and disapproval. These kids often develop a win-at-all-costs mentality and feel that whatever they do, it is never good enough. This feeling of inadequacy can affect all aspects of their lives.

The right balance

How involved should you be? Many parents look at their child's tennis as a joint venture, even to the extent of using the word "we" when discussing tennis. "No, I can't go out this weekend. 'We' have a tournament." No, "we" don't have a tournament, the child does!

Other parents go the other extreme and are totally uninvolved. They simply drop the kids off at the courts and pick them up an hour later. These parents view their role as that of activity directors. They book their kids' schedules, shuttle them from activity to activity, but rarely talk with them about what they're doing or make themselves available beyond the schedule.

I don't agree with either approach. One is too involved, the other not involved enough. You need to show your child that you care about his tennis and want to support him. But the trick is to support him without smothering him. It's a fine line, and it all begins with honest communication.

The first thing you need to communicate to your child is the reason that he is playing tennis. Then you must back that up with your actions.

Many parents tell their kids to "try hard and have fun," yet the first question those same parents ask when

"Son, the important thing is to have fun... did you win?"

their child walks in the door is "Did you win?" That question tells the child what's truly important to his parents—winning. When he wins, everything is wonderful. But when he loses, his parents often appear angry or disappointed with him.

Instead of asking your son if he won, when he walks in the door, ask how he played. Ask him what he learned and if he had fun. Make sure your questions and conversations tell him that "Johnny the tennis player" is separate from "Johnny the person."

Emphasize that his attitude and effort are what's important, and that the scoreboard does not record his worth. Teach him that wins and losses are significant only in how they are dealt with.

> *A child can never think a parent's level of affection is based on winning or losing.*
>
> Chris Evert
> 18-time Grand Slam singles champion

With this shift of emphasis, you create an entirely different world from that of the stereotypical "tennis parent." You're telling your child that having fun and learning are the most important aspects of his tennis. When the pressure of winning is taken away, he'll be better able to focus on learning, which translates into better tennis and a lot more fun.

The second part of successful communication is watching and listening. Is your child eager to go to tennis or is it a chore? Once there, pay attention to his body language. Does he look like he's having fun? Is he relating to the other kids and the instructor? Does he appear temperamental? Is he constantly looking up at you to see your reaction?

If you watch closely, he'll tell you what he wants out of tennis, what he is afraid of and how he feels about himself. He may not say it in words so you need to read between the lines.

Quite often children say what they feel their parents want to hear, rather than what's truly in their hearts. If your child feels that you'll listen to him without judging him, he'll be more open about expressing his feelings. You'll then be able to identify potential problems more easily.

To approach tennis with this attitude—and life, for that matter—you need to have your own act together. This means realizing that it's your child's time to shine and putting his needs ahead of your own.

In his book 101 Ways To Be A Terrific Sports Parent, Dr. Joel Fish offered eight warning signs for parents to be aware of that may signal that they're getting close to crossing the line between an involved and over-involved sports parent. If you:

1. Find yourself talking more about your child's sport than your child.
2. Are highly critical of your child's coach.
3. Talk to the child more like a coach than a parent i.e., always giving advice, instruction, and critiques.
4. Constantly tell your child to practice more.
5. Seem more emotionally invested in the sport than your child (i.e., you get more upset than he or she does about a lost game or performance mistake).
6. Get a great deal of status and prestige from your child's athletic accomplishments.
7. Believe that if your child just tried harder he or she could be successful in sport.

Speak with your child's pro about development and pleasure, not rankings or why he's not playing with the top kids. Ask the pro if he's making progress. Is he willing to listen to constructive criticism? How does he handle competition? Is he making friends? How does he feel about tennis, and about himself? Most important, ask if he is happy when he's playing.

Push aside those thoughts of a college scholarship or of dancing at the Wimbledon Ball. Except in very rare cases, tennis will never be more than a recreational activity in your child's life. If you treat it as such from the beginning, the chances of your son or daughter enjoying the game for many years will increase tremendously.

> *What kind of empty people need to validate themselves through the achievements of their children?*
>
> George Carlin
> Comedian

I've seen many promising players compete in junior tournaments, play for their high school and then never pick up a racket after their 18th birthday. Somewhere along the way the game stopped being fun. These kids burned out because of the pressure they felt to perform. Those kids are missing out on 50 or 60 years of fun and exercise playing tennis. It's very sad.

The relationship between a parent and a child is complex enough without the added stress of the "tennis parent syndrome." If there's tension within the relationship as a result of tennis, something is wrong. Provide guidance, unconditional love and support. Don't judge. Create an environment in which your child feels comfortable expressing himself, and be sure that you align your goals with his.

If your son's goal is to make his high school team, earn a tennis scholarship or make the pro tour, fine. Your job is to support him and provide him with the

> *I tell parents, if you're looking for a return on your investment, you're dead wrong.*
>
> Jim Loehr
> Sport psychologist

opportunity to reach his goal. If he simply wants to have fun, respect that and enjoy the game with him.

I'm often asked what advice I would give to parents and their children regarding tennis. To the kids I say simply, "Enjoy the game and let it take you where you want to go." To the parents I simply say, "Let them enjoy the ride."

Start the tradition

Everyday, on thousands of tennis courts around the globe, a countless number of senior citizens take the court with their adult children and grandchildren, hit a few balls and have the time of their lives.

These people, many of whom have been playing and enjoying tennis for 60 or 70 years, have accepted the gift of tennis, treasured it throughout their lives and passed it down to the next generation. This is tennis at its best, and the gift is yours to pass down to your children and grandchildren. Start the tradition now.

"WHEN IN DOUBT, CALL IT OUT."

These were the last words spoken during a conversation I overheard between a father and son before a junior tennis match.

When the father realized that I'd heard him, he laughed it off and said, "Hey, I was just kidding. Besides, it's tough out there." Hopefully, he was only joking, but even still, at one time or other we've all faced players we feel are giving us a raw deal with the line calls.

Whether it's a junior whose been instructed by parents or pros to "give nothing away", an adult who wants the ball to be out so badly that he actually sees an in ball as out, or a person simply making an honest mistake, the subject of bad line calls is always a sensitive one. Here are a few tips to help you and your child deal with an always sticky situation.

1. The first time it happens, there's not much you can do. It's their call, and the point stands. Let it slide and move on. Keep in mind that most people don't cheat and your opponent is much closer to the ball and in a better position to make the call than you.

Remember, a tennis ball is often traveling at an extremely fast speed, and since your opponent is usually running as she's making the call, it's easy to see how a mistake can be made. People deserve the benefit of the doubt.

2. If it happens again, and you truly feel it was a bad call, it's perfectly appropriate to take an extended look at where the ball bounced and ask them politely if they're sure of their call.

Don't be rude. Don't be sarcastic, and, above all, don't be confrontational. If you start out attacking them, they'll get defensive and it could get ugly. Let them know that you're paying attention and move on to the next point.

Give them a chance to take a second look and, if it was an honest mistake, allow them to correct it gracefully. Most players are honest and will want to make certain that they get it right. Many times the player will give you the point if you thought it was in.

3. If it happens a third time, continue to keep your composure, but become a bit more firm. If you're in a tournament, calmly walk up to the tournament desk and request a linesperson.

Most tournaments will provide you with a linesperson to settle any disputes. If, however, the tournament will not do that, you'll just have to deal with the bad calls and finish the match.

Don't lose your cool and let it destroy your game. A few bad calls here and there, though frustrating, probably won't alter the result of the match. For the "cheater" to be successful, he needs for you to lose your cool. Don't!

4. If it's a social game, simply finish the match. If you find that it's just too upsetting to continue, pack up your gear and leave. Tell your opponent that it's obviously a bad day since you can't agree on the calls. Call it a day, and tell him that you'll try it again another time.

This will get the message across that you're not going to tolerate the cheating. Play with her again and if you feel she's still cheating you, lose her phone number. It's not worth the aggravation.

Remember, it's not about the type of person they are— it's about the type of person you are and want your children to be!

Chapter 24

Beyond the Score

From the moment I struck my first tennis ball I knew that the game was special and that I wanted it to be a big part of my life, for the rest of my life. I've been fortunate to have that dream come true. You can as well.

The lessons I've offered in this book will not only improve your play but also the quality of your tennis life. You've seen that by simply making a few small adjustments, and learning to use your head, you can win many more matches with the strokes you have right now.

Whether you have a closet full of trophies or struggle to open a can of balls, there is a great joy to be found in the game. I sincerely hope that my book has given you some insights into making tennis one of the happiest parts of your life. I'd like to close by telling you about an old friend of mine who's found that happiness.

A tale of two players

Growing up, I had two best friends, John and Bill. The three of us did everything together. We hung out, went to the movies, talked about girls and complained about the usual things that kids complain about. Most of all, we played tennis.

Before, after, and sometimes instead of, school, we'd head over to the old lady's house down the street from where Bill lived. She had a cement court that had clearly seen better days: cracks extending from the net to the baseline and grass peeking up from in-between.

"Boy, that feels good!"

The conditions didn't matter. We just wanted to play. And play we did.

For hours each week, John, Bill and I ruled that court as the greatest tennis players in the world. We played the French, Australian and, when the gardener had neglected the grass in the cracks, Wimbledon and the U.S. Open. Davis Cup? You'd better believe it! We had our red, white and blue t-shirts and, several times each week, we triumphantly brought the Cup back to the United States.

We became our favorite pros. I was always Rod Laver. It didn't matter that the "Rocket" was left-handed and I was a "rightie," he was my guy. John was John Newcombe. First, because his name was John but mostly because, among the three of us, he was the only one who had a chance of growing a Newcombe-like moustache. Bill, the clown of our little trio, was Illie Nastase.

We battled each other over hundreds of matches, hitting thousands of balls in the court, out of the court and, on occasion, into the old lady's pool. She'd look out her window, feign aggravation and soon after bring us a pitcher of lemonade. We'd sit under her big oak tree, drink our lemonade and talk about our matches and other things.

I was a pretty good player. John was better than me and extremely competitive, with dreams of playing pro tennis. Bill was better than no one. Tall, thin and painfully un-athletic, the Nastase of our little group struggled to make contact with the ball and when he did, it usually seemed to rest in the deep end of the pool. "Bagel Bill" we called him due to the number of games he usually won each set. But it never mattered who was better, we were just having fun.

John and I also played "real" tennis: the junior tournament circuit, and for our school teams. Bill would always be at our matches, cheering us on.

Sadly, as often happens with high school graduation, the tremendous trio drifted apart. I went to school in Florida, John to California and no one was ever quite sure what happened to Bill after high school.

The years went by and I often thought back to those great times on that horrible tennis court. Whatever happened to my buddies? Where were they? What were they doing? Were they married? Did they have kids? Most of all, I wondered if they still played tennis.

They had to, I assumed. It was such an important part of our lives growing up. How could they not? I certainly had continued my love of the game. After tennis I began to teach and write about the sport. Surely, my buddies were still involved in some way. I decided to find out.

> Competition must be focused on the process of what you are doing, rather than the result of that effort, the so-called winning or losing.
>
> John Wooden
> Legendary UCLA basketball coach

Thanks to a few phone calls and the Internet, I was able to track down my long-lost friends. Both had ventured out into the world after college but had eventually returned and settled close to where we grew up.

I picked up the phone and called John first. He seemed genuinely happy to hear from me and we caught up on the years quickly. John never played professional tennis but his competitive nature had served him well in the world of business.

I then asked if he still played tennis. His voice dropped and developed a bit of an edge to it. "No," he said firmly. "I haven't picked up a racket since my freshman year in college."

The tone in his voice warned me not to question further but, deciding not to mind my own business, I said, "Why not?"

The phone was silent for a moment and then John explained, "I got to college, went out for the tennis team and found that the high school tennis star really wasn't very good after all. I couldn't beat anyone so I gave my rackets away and haven't played since."

"Do you miss it?" I asked. "No, I've moved on," John answered, a little too quickly. "Moved on" clearly meant "grown up." After a few more minutes, we said goodbye, promising to get the families together.

Bill, coincidently, showed up at the club one day. I had just come off the court and there he was at the front desk checking out our programs. It turns out he'd just moved back to the area and was looking for a place to play tennis.

We reminisced a bit and I told him I was glad to see that he was still playing tennis. "I still stink," he said with a smile, "but I play three to four times a week and absolutely love it." We made plans to get together over the weekend to hit a few balls.

A few days later, we took the court and Bill was right, he did still stink (just kidding, Bill). Actually, he was a 2.5 level player. He ran after everything, hit some nice shots, made many more errors, but clearly loved every minute of it.

We came off the court and, over a soda, talked about my conversation with John. I told him how interesting it was that, of my two great friends, John had quit tennis while "Bagel Bill" was still madly in love with the game. Bill said that he wasn't particularly surprised. "Though we both played the same game, it meant different things to each of us," he said. "John liked tennis because he won so much," Bill went on.

> *The moment of victory is far too short to live for that and nothing else.*
>
> Martina Navratilova
> 18-time Grand Slam singles champion

"Once the winning stopped, the game brought him no pleasure so why would he keep playing? For me," he continued, "the results of matches were never an issue so I learned to enjoy other aspects of the game. I love the workout, the socializing and the chance to work on improving my skills."

At his old club, Bill took a private lesson on Mondays and became great friends with his pro. He attended a Cardio Tennis class on Wednesdays where he made friends and, in fact, met his fiancée. On Sundays, he and a friend rented a court and drilled and, when they finished, they'd go out for breakfast. I mentioned to Bill that it was interesting that there was no competition involved in any of his tennis.

A higher level of competition

"That's not true," he said. "I compete every time I step onto the court. During my lessons and practice sessions, I work on trying to make my strokes and footwork better than they were the previous week. At my Cardio Tennis classes I try to become fitter. I'm competing with myself and my level from the previous time I played.

I know that most tennis players are more gifted athletically than I am, so there's no point in comparing myself to them. I'm well aware of my level and have learned to judge my progress, and find my enjoyment, from things other than the score of a match."

Bill is a perfect example of a player who, in all probability, will never advance beyond the lower levels of tennis and is looked down upon by the tennis snobs of the world. He truly couldn't care less. He loves tennis and gets a tremendous amount of satisfaction from his time on the court.

Would Bill's attitude change if he were a gifted athlete? I don't think so. Bill is a champion chess player but only talks about the interesting moves that came up during his games. I've never heard him mention the results of his games. He truly loves the "process" of both games and learns from them in ways that have nothing to do with wins or losses. You can, too.

There is a level of winning beyond the score and there's no rule that says you have to buy into the kill-or-be-killed culture when you step onto the tennis court. While competing against others can offer many positive attributes, it can also be extremely stressful, and more and more players are finding that they have enough stress in their lives and want a break from it during their recreation time. Bob Stiller is one of those players.

Stiller, CEO of the Green Mountain Coffee Company and Forbes Magazine "Entrepreneur of the Year" in 2001, views his time on the court as a physical and psychological massage. "We all need variety in our lives and tennis, for me, refreshes my mind and body. I don't feel the need to outscore someone to gain that refreshment. Winning on or off the tennis court is about knowing and appreciating yourself while working to realize your goals—whatever they may be."

If you feel that your skills are not up to par or you're simply not interested in the pressure that can accompany competitive tennis, stay away from it. Take lessons, attend classes and compete with yourself. Take a look at where you are, set a realistic goal for where you'd like to be and enjoy trying to narrow the gap between the two.

When you adopt this approach, a moment will come when hitting the ball cleanly will mean more to you than the outcome of a match. You will then be my definition of the winning-est tennis player ever!

The only regret I have is the feeling that I will die without having played enough tennis.

Jean Borotra
Five-time Grand Slam singles champion

Appendix A

USTA Tennis Rating Program (NTRP)

1.0: You are a complete beginner

1.5: You have limited experience and are working primarily on getting the ball in play.

2.0: You lack court experience and your strokes need developing. You are familiar with the basic positions for singles and doubles play.

2.5: You are learning to judge where the ball is going, although your court coverage is limited. You can sustain a short rally of slow pace with other players of the same ability.

3.0: You are fairly consistent when hitting medium-paced shots, but are not comfortable with all strokes and lack execution when trying for directional control, depth, or power. Your most common doubles formation is one-up, one-back.

3.5: You have achieved improved stroke dependability with directional control on moderate shots, but need to develop depth and variety. You exhibit more aggressive net play, have improved court coverage and are developing teamwork in doubles.

4.0: You have dependable strokes, including directional control and depth on both forehand and backhand sides on moderate-paced shots. You can use lobs, overheads, approach shots and volleys with some success and occasionally force errors when serving. Rallies may be lost due to impatience. Teamwork in doubles is evident.

4.5: You have developed your use of power and spin and can handle pace. You have sound footwork, can control depth of shots, and attempt to vary game plan according to your opponents. You can hit first serves with power and accuracy and place the second serve. You tend to overhit on difficult shots. Aggressive net play is common in doubles.

5.0: You have good shot anticipation and frequently have an outstanding shot or attribute around which a game may be structured. You can regularly hit winners or force errors off of short balls and can put away volleys. You can successfully execute lobs, drop shots, half volleys, overhead smashes, and have good depth and spin on most second serves.

5.5: You have mastered power and/or consistency as a major weapon. You can vary strategies and styles of play in a competitive situation and hit dependable shots in a stress situation.

6.0 to 7.0: You have had intensive training for national tournament competition at the junior and collegiate levels and have obtained a sectional and/or national ranking.

7.0: You are a world-class player.

More info: usta.com

Appendix B

Tennis Skills Inventory

Write a few brief sentences in each section. This is for your own benefit, so you can see which areas you need to work on.

Forehand	
Backhand	
Volleys	
Overhead	
Serve	
Return of serve	
Fitness: strength, agility, endurance and flexibility.	
Mental game: Ability to concentrate, control temper, fight back when playing poorly or when behind, ability to put forth a consistent effort both in practice and play.	

USE THIS INVENTORY AS A LEARNING TOOL TO EVALUATE YOUR GAME.

Appendix C

Goals Program

Here is an example of a Goals Program for one of my students whose long-term goal was to make her high school tennis team.

Name: Elizabeth Jones
Long-Term Goal: In six months, to make the Central High School tennis team.
Short-Term Goals: 1st three months: improve overall consistency and footwork.
                    2nd three months: improve match play.

Course Of Action:

To develop consistency

For the next three months, play tennis at least twice a week and work on consistency drills for all aspects of your game. Do a lot of crosscourt and down-the-line drills. Try to get to the point where you can keep the ball going 25-30 times each way. The goal is to develop the ability to keep the ball in play for an extended period of time, so hit at whatever pace you need to keep the ball going. Don't sacrifice control for power. Practice NOT making errors! Also practice your serve. Hit at least one basket every time you practice. Set up targets in the service box; consistency and control are much more important than power.

To improve movement

Begin an off-court training program that includes both endurance and agility exercises.

Endurance: Run for 30 minutes, three times a week. Go as fast or as slow as you need to to complete the time. Build up to 30 minutes if too difficult.

Agility: Jump rope on the days you don't do your endurance training. Begin by jumping with both feet, and then just the left foot, then the right, and then alternating feet. Build up to the following:
- 50 jumps with both feet
- 50 jumps on the left foot
- 50 jumps on the right foot
- 50 jumps alternating feet

To improve match play:

Start playing practice sets and matches. Try to play an extra time or two a week. A perfect playing schedule might be one lesson, then one practice session to work on strokes and consistency, and finally one or two practice matches each week.

Appendix D

Grips Of The Game

As an easy reference, lay your racket on edge and imagine the butt cap of the racket is the face of the clock.

Name	How to find it	Advantages	Disadvantages
EASTERN FOREHAND	Shake hands with the racket. The "meat" of your palm should be behind the handle at approximately 3:00.	All-purpose grip which can be used for both forehands and backhands as well as forehand volleys.	Difficult to hit topspin due to the flat nature of the racket face. Unstable for backhand volleys. Hitting high bouncing balls can be difficult.
WESTERN FOREHAND	From the Eastern grip, move your hand clockwise or to the right (for a right-hander). The knuckles of your index finger should be on the bottom of the handle, pointing to the ground at approximately 6:00.	Closes the racket face, which produces more topspin. Topspin allows you to hit the ball harder and maintain control.	Requires a great deal of athleticism to control the racket face Very difficult on low bouncing and wide shots. Cannot volley with this grip. Makes hitting slice and drop shots extremely difficult

SEMI-WESTERN FOREHAND	In-between Eastern and Western forehands. Index knuckle is at approx. 4:00.	Versatile grip with which you can hit topspin, flat and even slice. Good for hitting high balls.	Difficult to hit volleys. Drop shots are very awkward to hit.
EASTERN BACKHAND	From the Eastern forehand, turn your hand counter-clockwise The knuckle of your index finger should be on the inside bevel of the handle at approx. 12:00.	Great for flat or topspin backhands.	Slicing the ball is difficult
CONTINENTAL	Mid-way between Eastern forehand and Eastern backhand grips. Knuckle of index finger is at approx. 1:00.	Great for hitting volleys, spin serves, overheads, slice backhands and forehands, drop shots, low balls and two-handed backhands.	Difficult to hit topspin on ground-strokes. High shots are difficult unless you use slice.

Appendix E

Unforced Error Match Statistics

_____VS._____

SET #_____

Game 1	Game 1
Game 2	Game 2
Game 3	Game 3
Game 4	Game 4
Game 5	Game 5
Game 6	Game 6
Game 7	Game 7
Game 8	Game 8
Game 9	Game 9
Game 10	Game 10
Game 11	Game 11
Game 12	Game 12
Tiebreaker	Tiebreaker

FH: Forehand error	**BH**: Backhand error	**V**: Volley error
OVH: Overhead error	**S**: Double fault	**E**: Effort error

Select References

- Vic Braden, *Tennis 2000*, Revised edition 1998, Little Brown & Co.

- Peter Burwash, *Tennis for Life*, 1982, Times Books

- Brad Gilbert, *Winning Ugly*, 1994, Fireside.

- Donald Chu, *Power Tennis Training*, 1994, Human Kinetics.

- Paul Fein, *Tennis Confidential*, 2002, Brassey's, Inc.

- John McEnroe, *You Cannot Be Serious*, 2002, Penguin Putnam Inc.

- Dr. John F. Murray, *Smart Tennis*, 1999, Jossey-Bass.

- Dr. Andrew Weil, *Healthy Aging*, 2005, Knopf.

- Joel Drucker, *Jimmy Connors Saved My Life*, 2004, Sport Classic Books.

- Anthony Robbins, *Awaken the Giant Within*, 1992, Free Press.

- George Sheehan, *Personal Best*, 1989, Rodale Press.

- Dr. Michael F. Roizen & Dr. Mehmet C. Oz, *You: The Owner's Manual*, 2005, Harper Resource.

- Jeff Greenwald, *Fearless Tennis: The 5 Mental Keys to Unlocking Your Potential* (Audio CD), 2002, Mental Edge Intl.

- Dr. Joel Fish, *101 Ways to be a Terrific Sports Parent*, 2003, Fireside.

Credits

- Dr. Andrew Weil quote from *Healthy Aging* permission of Dr. Weil
- Quote from *Coaching Tennis* by permission of Chuck Kriese
- Permission by Bill Mountford granted for personal quotes
- Permission by Geoff Norton granted for personal quotes
- Permission by Sammy Samson granted for personal quotes
- Excerpts from *Jimmy Connors Saved My Life* as permitted by Joel Drucker
- Direct quote of Dr. John F. Murray (www.johnmurray.com) permission of Dr. Murray
- Permission by Ken DeHart granted for personal quotes
- Excerpts from *Tennis Confidential* as permitted by Paul Fein
- Excerpts from *Tennis Mind* as permitted by Dr. Robert Heller
- Quote from www.worldoflaughtertour.com as permitted by Steve Wilson
- Excerpts from www.tenniswarrior.com as permitted by Tom Veneziano
- Article from January 2006 *TIME* Magazine article as permitted by *TIME*
- Quotes from US Racquet Stringers Association (www.usra.com) granted by David Bone
- Direct quote of Dr. Andrews Bazos with permission granted by Dr. Bazos
- Personal quote of Bob Stiller with permission granted by Mr. Stiller

Index

Acknowledgments

First and foremost, special thanks go to my parents for giving me the gift of tennis and so much more.

The journey that resulted in this book has truly been a team effort. I'd like to thank the members of my "team" for helping to make my publishing dream a reality: Paul Fein, Donna Doherty, Uday Kumar, Maureen Malliaras, Pamela Garrett, and the wonderful people at Mansion Grove House. Also, Scott Hazlewood, Kris Moran, Jacques De Spoelberch and Norman Zeitchick.

And those whose knowledge and kindness inspired the words that filled these pages: Dr. Andrew Bazos, Ray Benton, Vic Braden, David Bone, Ken DeHart, Joel Drucker, Scott Ford, Dr. Robert Heller, Cliff Kurtzman, James Martin, Bob Mitchell, Jack Mitchell, Barbara Morgan, Bill Mountford, Rick Murray, Dr. John F. Murrray, Geoff Norton, Milton Ossorio, Kevin Quarantello, Zane Saul, Bob Stiller, Tom Veneziano, Stephen Wilkes, Brent Zeller. To Barbara "Bobbie" Kruk who will always remain in our hearts.

And, finally, thanks to everyone who's ever shared a tennis court with me. Win or lose, it's always fun!

Greg Moran
greg_moran@TennisBeyondBigShots.com

Want More?

Greg's Beyond Clinic:

Go to TennisBeyondBigShots.com and discover new ways that Greg can get you on the fast track to top tennis performance. Plus more!

TennisBeyondBigShots.com

Consumer Copies:

Go to TennisBeyondBigShots.com for a current list of Retailers and discount offers for copies of Tennis Beyond Big Shots. Also available through leading chain and independent bookstores, online retailers, tennis pro shops, sporting goods stores, and catalogs.

TennisBeyondBigShots.com

Reseller Copies:

Distributor, Retailer & Tennis Group Inquiries to
- Website: mansiongrovehouse.com
- Email: sales@mansiongrovehouse.com
- Phone: 408.404.7277
- Fax: 408.404.7277

Big Smiling Series

ISBN 1932421114
2006 Second Edition

Raising Big Smiling Tennis Kids

Whether you are a tennis playing parent or a parent curious about tennis, this book will empower you to raise kids who swing the tennis racket with as much aplomb as their happy smiles.

The best age to get your kid started in tennis. How to motivate kids to go back, practice after practice. When to focus exclusively on tennis. Save on lessons, find scholarships and sponsors. How to pursue a career in professional tennis. Gain insight into tennis organizations and agents. Have fun along the way at the best tennis camps and resorts.

Raising Big Smiling Squash Kids

Stanford University recently added Squash to its athletics, joining Yale and Cornell. Forbes magazine rates Squash as the number one sport for fitness. With courts and college programs springing up across the country, the opportunities for a first class education are enhanced like never before for the serious junior squash player. Richard Millman, world-class coach and Georgetta Morque, a prolific sportswriter, offer a complete roadmap for parents, professionals and kids. The best age to get started in squash; how to motivate kids; the road to top colleges; and attractive career options. Plus: cultivating friendships, character building and achieving a lifetime of fitness.

ISBN 1932421432
2006 First Edition

Available Worldwide

Printed in the United States
85151LV00001B/55-84/A